IT Today

IT Today

McGraw-Hill

Boston   Burr Ridge, IL   Dubuque, IA   Madison, WI   New York   San Francisco   St. Louis
Bangkok   Bogotá   Caracas   Lisbon   London   Madrid
Mexico City   Milan   New Delhi   Seoul   Singapore   Sydney   Taipei   Toronto

McGraw-Hill Higher Education

A Division of The McGraw-Hill Companies

IT TODAY

Published by McGraw-Hill, an imprint of The McGraw-Hill Companies, Inc.
1221 Avenue of the Americas, New York, NY, 10020.

Some ancillaries, including electronic and print components, may not be available to
customers outside the United States.

This book is printed on acid-free paper.

3 4 5 6 7 8 9 0   QPD/QPD   0 9 8 7 6 5 4 3 2

ISBN 0-07-242261-0

Vice president and editorial director: *Michael W. Junior*
Senior sponsoring editor: *Jodi McPherson*
Editorial coordinator: *Alexandra Arnold*
Senior marketing manager: *Jeff Parr*
Senior project manager: *Susan Trentacosti*
Senior production supervisor: *Lori Koetters*
Senior designer: *Laurie J. Entringer*
Senior supplement coordinator: *Marc Mattson*
New media project manager: *David Barrick*
Cover design: *Asylum Studios*
Interior design: *Asylum Studios*
Compositor: *Cecelia G. Morales*
Typeface: *10/14 Cochin*
Printer: *Quebecor Printing Book Group/Dubuque*

Library of Congress Card Number: 00-105723

www.mhhe.com

about IT Today . . .

In October 1999, McGraw-Hill/Irwin invited 16 college professors from across the country to join in an annual Information Technology Advisory Panel (ITAP). One of the top ideas exchanged revolved around the creation of a new computer literacy book. Our ITAP members indicated that things are changing and that technology products need to find a way to engage students in a meaningful dialogue that demonstrates topics relevant to them as students and as technology users.

At McGraw-Hill, we decided to take this idea to heart. We hired Jack Rochester as a writer and consultant to distill the ITAP comments and feedback. Our ITAP members suggested that as the need for computer literacy continues to grow, so too does the definition and the dynamic classroom for teaching and learning. As a result, we took this feedback to several focus groups and additional IT Advisory Panels, and found they all agreed on similar coverage, similar themes, and a new concept for teaching literacy. We call it *IT Today.*

Jack Rochester
Consultant/Writer

Information Technology Advisory Panel Members

Judy Cameron, *Spokane Community College*
Ray Cone, *Odessa College*
Pat Coulter, *Pennsylvania College of Technology*
Kevin Croteau, *Francis Marion University*
Jacquelyn Crowe, *Spokane Community College*
Rory DeSimone, *University of Florida–Gainesville*
Bret Dickey, *Spokane Community College*
Susan Fry, *Boise State University*
Gail Gemberling, *University of Texas–Austin*
Nancy Goettel, *Coastal Carolina University*
Laurel Helm, *Eastern Washington University*
Michelle Hulett, *Southwest Missouri State University*
Kathy Jesiolowski, *Milwaukee Area Technical College*
Kurt Kominek, *Northeast State Technical Community College*
Denise Leete, *Pennsylvania College of Technology*
Linda Lynam, *Central Missouri State University*
Donna Madsen, *Kirkwood Community College*
Daniella Marghitu, *Auburn University*
Phil Marshall, *University of South Carolina*
Linda Mehlinger, *Morgan State University*
Barbara Miller, *Indiana University–Bloomington*
Pat Ormand, *Utah Valley State*
Woody Pekoske, *North Carolina State University*
Alan Rea, *Western Michigan University*
Corey Schou, *Idaho State*
Dick Schwartz, *Macomb Community College*
Margaret Thomas, *Ohio University*
Suzanne Tomlinson, *Iowa State*

INFORMATION TECHNOLOGY AT MCGRAW-HILL/IRWIN

At McGraw-Hill Higher Education, we publish instructional materials targeted at the higher education market. In an effort to expand the tools of higher learning, we publish texts, lab manuals, study guides, testing materials, software, and multimedia products.

At McGraw-Hill/Irwin (a division of McGraw-Hill Higher Education), we realize that technology has created and will continue to create new mediums for professors and students to use in managing resources and communicating information to one another. We strive to provide the most flexible and complete teaching and learning tools available, as well as offer solutions to the changing world of teaching and learning.

 McGraw-Hill/Irwin is dedicated to providing the tools for today's instructors and students to successfully navigate the world of Information Technology.

- **Seminar series** — McGraw-Hill/Irwin's Technology Connection seminar series offered across the country every year demonstrates the latest technology products and encourages collaboration among teaching professionals.

- **McGraw-Hill/Osborne** — This division of The McGraw-Hill Companies is known for its best-selling Internet titles, *Harley Hahn's Internet & Web Yellow Pages* and the *Internet Complete Reference*. For more information, visit Osborne at **www.osborne.com.**

- **Digital solutions** — McGraw-Hill/Irwin is committed to publishing digital solutions. Taking your course online doesn't have to be a solitary venture, nor does it have to be a difficult one. We offer several solutions that will allow you to enjoy all the benefits of having your course material online. For more information, visit **www.mhhe.com/solutions/index.mhtml.**

- **Packaging options** — For more information about our discount options, contact your McGraw-Hill/Irwin Sales representative at 1-800-338-3987 or visit our website at **www.mhhe.com/it.**

McGraw-Hill's IT Today

THE IT TODAY STORY...CREATED BY THE MARKET, FOR THE MARKET.

✔ Develop A New Computer Concepts Text

At McGraw-Hill/Irwin, we take market feedback very seriously. So seriously that when a group of 16 college professors from across the country told us to develop a new computer concepts product because their needs were changing—we listened.

Our Information Technology Advisory Panel (ITAP) met in Park City, Utah, in October, 1999 and they told us to rethink the way computer concepts books are created. Things like—have fewer pages and get to the heart of the materials. Things like—give it a consumer theme. Kids today are buying and upgrading computers, and they are technology consumers—cover the traditional needs (hardware, software, telecommunications)—and cover it with those themes in mind.

✔ Make IT Short

Our market feedback and focus groups indicated that some books are just too long. The need for really brief coverage for the computer literacy course is here, especially with the rise of applications (MS Office) coverage in the literacy course.

✔ Start from Scratch

Do it right from the beginning. That's what they told us. Trying to fit an existing product into this 100-page, brief coverage of concepts is tough. This needs to be a new product created with the themes needed to keep students interested, the topics to develop their computer literacy, and created in 100 pages or so.

✔ Give Top 5 Chapter Coverage

Independent focus groups of professors in two- and four-year programs agreed—I need to cover the topics that will make my student computer literate and able to be a knowledgeable consumer of technology:

1. Using Computers
2. Using the Internet
3. Using Software
4. Using Hardware
5. Using Communications Technology

✔ Round IT Out with a CD-ROM

Some people also indicated that just in case the book coverage was not enough, we needed to provide a CD-ROM and website to supplement coverage—not just repeat what's in the book, but add depth and breadth to the topics covered.

In addition to adding more content on the CD-ROM and website links, we are integrating interactive exercises on difficult topics, such as storage and binary numbers, on the CD-ROM so students can enhance and expand their skills. The CD-ROM will also include an assessment program so professors and students can evaluate their progress. This CD-ROM will be topically driven to maximize flexibility and usage, and it will stand alone from the book. That is, if you want to use it with the book you can, but the book and CD-ROM are not dependent on each other. They complement one another.

✔ Give IT a Technology Consumer Theme

Our opening vignette will be a PC advertisement to introduce students to key terms and things that they will need to know when buying or upgrading a PC. In addition, a "PC & You" running feature will be included throughout the book to show how the chapter material relates to buying/upgrading a PC.

According to the members of ITAP, all students are consumers of Technology and in introducing them to the topics of computer literacy (hardware/software/telecommunications), we should keep in mind the "E" in everything electronic—why E matters to *them*. So we are sticking to the key topics and offering E-spective on important points.

IT TODAY...JUST ONE PART OF MCGRAW-HILL'S TOTAL SOLUTION

TEXT FEATURES:

✔ *Chapter Openers.* The opening vignettes are designed to peak student interest in the chapter content:

"It used to be that peripherals were a keyboard, a mouse, a monitor, a printer. And while we still need all of them, we can now select from a vast array of peripherals that extend the PC's usefulness, from a microphone to issue voice commands to a surround sound speaker system to listen to CDs while we compute. Two innovative peripherals are the Hewlett-Packard CapShare, a portable scanner and copier that lets you store, view, and send information to others. The other is the S3 Rio MP3 player, which captures and stores MP3 files and plays them back. Move over, Walkman! (Chapter 4).

✔ *PC & You.* These call-out boxes keep the theme of buying and upgrading a PC going throughout the chapters and feature specific actions and questions students will run into, as well as possible solutions. Most students will at some point in their lifetime be faced with the buying or upgrading of a computer. To maintain their interest in why the terminology, software, and hardware are important, we've chosen to add the "PC & You" to illustrate right on the spot why what they are learning matters to them:

The Web is a great place to buy a PC. You can get answers to your questions, look at many brands and models, and compare prices. You can select a prepackaged system or save some money by buying a refurbished computer. Perhaps best of all, you can design, or configure, your own system. The Web is visual and interactive, so you can explore the options and learn more about each one. If you've set a limit on how much you want to spend, you can update the system price as you add or change components.

✔ *E-Notes.* A running "Post-it" style note that emphasizes the "E" factor in everything covered in the text: how electronic everything has become and the significance and impact of the Web in students' lives. The practical flavor of "E-notes" is meant to engage students and generate the "Oh, I know what you mean" response in students:

> **E-Notes**
> Faster mail is better mail.

"The total (number of e-mail accounts is over) four hundred million. In fact, in 1995, the amount of electronic mail delivered in the United States surpassed the amount of "snail" mail printed on paper and handled by the United States Postal Service . . . . E-mail matters."

— Michael Specter, "Your Mail Has Vanished," *The New Yorker,* December 6, 1999, p. 95.

✔ *Learning the Lingo.* By calling out key terms in "Learning the Lingo," we want to help students identify key terminology important to their goals of buying or upgrading a computer and becoming digital consumers, as well as the goal of the course—achieving computer literacy:

> **LEARNING THE *lingo***
>
> **search engine** A type of software application that locates key words or phrases on the Web.

✔ *Talking Issues.* Perhaps one of our most important features according to market feedback, "Talking Issues" illustrates to students the reality behind the world of Information Technology. "Talking Issues" is designed to show the implications and challenges students will face with decision making, as well as the implications of such situations and decisions:

> **talking*issues***
>
> **WHO CAN READ YOUR E-MAIL?**
>
> Who can read your e-mail? Just about anyone. According to Tara Lemmey, director of the Electronic Frontier Foundation (www.eff.org), your e-mail messages are about as secure as sending a postcard through the mail. If you work for someone and use their computer system to send e-mail, your employer has the right to read your messages.

RESOURCES FOR INSTRUCTORS

We understand that, in today's teaching environment, offering a textbook alone is not sufficient to meet the needs of the many instructors who use our books. To teach effectively, instructors must have a full complement of supplemental resources to assist them in every facet of teaching, from preparing for class to conducting a lecture to assessing students' comprehension. *IT Today* offers a complete, fully integrated supplements package and website, as described below.

Instructor's Resource Kit

The Instructor's Resource Kit is a CD-ROM, containing the Instructor's Manual in both MS Word and .pdf formats, PowerPoint slides, Brownstone test generating software, and accompanying test item files for each chapter. The features of each component of the Instructor's Resource Kit are highlighted below.

- **Instructor's Manual.** Prepared by Linda Mehlinger of Morgan State University, the Instructor's Manual contains a schedule showing how much time is required to cover the material in the chapter, a list of the chapter competencies and key terms, a Chapter Outline with lecture notes, a list of numbered figures in the text, and suggested exercises. Also included are answers to all the exercises in the chapter review section and answers to On the Web exercises. It also contains a helpful introduction that explains the features, benefits, and suggested uses of the IM.

- **PowerPoint Presentation.** Prepared by Suzanne Tomlinson of Iowa State University, the PowerPoint presentation is designed to provide instructors with a comprehensive teaching resource and includes key terms and definitions, concept overviews, figures from the text, additional examples/illustrations, anticipated student questions with answers, discussion topics, and Concept Checks. Included with the presentation are comprehensive speaker's notes.

- **Computerized Test Bank.** Prepared by Bill and Sharon Daley of the University of Oregon, the *IT Today* test bank contains a series of questions categorized by topic and level of learning (definition, concept, and application). This same learning scheme is introduced in the website to provide a valuable testing and reinforcement

tool. Each question is assigned a category: Level 1—definition, Level 2—concept, and Level 3—application. A test item table is provided for each chapter to give instructors a quick overview of the number and type of questions for each section in a chapter.

Interactive Companion CD-ROM

This free student CD-ROM, designed for use in class, in the lab, or at home by students and professors alike, includes a collection of interactive tutorial labs on some of the most popular and difficult concepts topics to illustrate in information technology. By combining video, interactive exercises, animation, additional content, and actual "lab" tutorials, we expand the reach and scope of the textbook. The lab titles are listed below:

Available Now:
- Computer Anatomy
- Binary Numbers
- Storage
- E-Mail
- Learning to Program I
- Learning to Program II
- Network Communications
- Intro to Multimedia
- Databases
- Workplace Issues (ergonomics/privacy/security)

Coming Soon:
- User Interfaces
- Photo Editing
- Word Processing
- Spreadsheets
- Directories, Folders, Files
- Using Files
- CPU Simulator
- Troubleshooting
- Web Pages and Html
- SQL Queries

Digital Solutions to Help You Manage Your Course

- **PageOut.** PageOut is our Course Website Development Center that offers a syllabus page, URL, McGraw-Hill Online Learning Center content, online exercises and quizzes, gradebook, discussion board, and an area for student Web pages.

Available for free with any McGraw-Hill/Irwin product, PageOut requires no prior knowledge of HTML, no long hours of coding, and a way for course coordinators and professors to provide a full-course website. PageOut offers a series of templates—simply fill them with your course information and click on one of 16 designs. The process takes under an hour and leaves you with a **professionally designed website.** We'll even get you started with sample websites, or enter your syllabus for you! PageOut is so straightforward and intuitive, it's little wonder why over 12,000 college professors are using it.

For more information, visit the PageOut website at **www.pageout.net.**

- *Online Learning Centers/Websites.* The Online Learning Center (OLC) Website that accompanies *IT Today* is accessible through our Information Technology Supersite at **www.mhhe.com/it** or at the book site **www.mhhe.com/cit/ittoday.** This site provides additional learning and instructional tools developed using the same three-level approach found in the text and supplements to offer a consistent method for students to enhance their comprehension of the concepts presented in the text. The OLC/Website is divided into these three levels:

  Level 1: Includes tips and tricks, FAQs, expanded book features such as "PC & You," and more *must know* items that interest students with hyperlinks and extended examples.

  Level 2: Includes additional quizzes for students to test their knowledge and skills. In our student focus groups across the county, students indicated this was a key piece of the website that increases their ability to be successful in class.

  Level 3: Includes additional exercises and hands-on projects/activities in the following categories:
  - Teamwork
  - Ethics
  - Buying a PC
  - Privacy and Security
  - Careers and the Impact of IT

- **Online Courses Available.** Online Learning Centers (OLCs) are your perfect solutions for Internet-based content. Simply put, these Centers are "digital cartridges" that contain a book's pedagogy and supplements. As students read the book, they can go online and take self-grading quizzes or work through interactive exercises. These also provide students appropriate access to lecture materials and other key supplements.

Online Learning Centers can be delivered through any of these platforms:
- McGraw-Hill Learning Architecture (TopClass)
- Blackboard.com
- ecollege.com (formally Real Education)
- WebCT (a product of Universal Learning Technology)

McGraw-Hill has partnerships with **WebCT** and **Blackboard** to make it even easier to take your course online. Now you can have McGraw-Hill content delivered through the leading Internet-based learning tool for higher education.

At McGraw-Hill, we have the following service agreements with **WebCT** and **Blackboard:**

- Instructor Advantage
  Instructor Advantage is a special level of service McGraw-Hill offers in conjuction with WebCT designed to help you get up and running with your new course. A **team of specialists** will be immediately available to ensure everything **runs smoothly** through the **life** of your adoption.

- Instructor Advantage Plus
  Qualified McGraw-Hill adopters will be eligible for an even higher level of service. A **certified WebCT or Blackboard specialist** will provide a full day of **on-site training** for you and your staff. You will then have **unlimited** e-mail and phone support through the life of your adoption. Please contact your local McGraw-Hill representative for more details.

Technology Connection Seminar Series

McGraw-Hill/Irwin's Technology Connection seminar series offered across the country every year demonstrates the latest technology products and encourages collaboration among teaching professionals.

MS Office 2000 Applications Texts and CDs

Available separately, or packaged with *IT Today,* McGraw-Hill offers three applications series: The O'Leary Series, The Advantage Series, or The Interactive Computing Series. Each series features its own unique approach to teaching MS Office in order to meet the needs of a variety of students and course goals.

- *The O'Leary Series* features a project-based, visual, step-by-step walkthrough of applications.

- *The Advantage Series* features a case-based, what, why, and how approach to learning applications to enhance critical thinking skills.

- *The Interactive Computing Series* features a visual, two-page spread to provide a more skills-based approach to learning applications.

Each series offers Microsoft Office User Specialist (MOUS) approved courseware to signify that it has been independently reviewed and approved in complying with the standards of content coverage related to the Microsoft Exams and Certification Program. For more information on Microsoft's MOUS certification program, please visit Microsoft's website at: **www.microsoft.com/office/traincert/.**

Also available for applications are the *Interactive Computing Series* Computer-Based Training CD-ROM tutorials. These CD-ROMs offer a visual, interactive way to develop and apply software skills. The CD-ROM features a unique "skills-concepts-steps" approach, and includes interactive exercises and performance-based assessment. These CD-ROMs are simulated, so there is no need for the actual software package on the computer.

Skills Assessment

McGraw-Hill/Irwin offers two innovative systems to meet your skills assessment needs. These two products are available for use with any of our applications manual series.

- **ATLAS** (Active Technology Learning Assessment System) is one option to consider for an application skills assessment tool from McGraw-Hill. ATLAS allows students to perform tasks while working live within the Microsoft applications environment. ATLAS provides flexibility for you in your course by offering:

  - Pretesting options
  - Posttesting options
  - Course placement testing
  - Diagnostic capabilities to reinforce skills
  - Proficiency testing to measure skills
  - ATLAS is Web-enabled, customizable, and is available for Microsoft Office 2000.

- **SimNet** (Simulated Network Assessment Product) is another option for a skills assessment tool that permits you to test students' software skills in a simulated environment. SimNet is available for Microsoft Office 97 (deliverable via a network) and Microsoft Office 2000 (deliverable via a network and the Web). SimNet provides flexibility for you in your course by offering:

  - Pretesting options
  - Posttesting options
  - Course placement testing
  - Diagnostic capabilities to reinforce skills
  - Proficiency testing to measure skills

For more information on either skills assessment software, please contact your local sales representative, or visit us at **www.mhhe.com/it.**

PowerWeb for Concepts

PowerWeb is an exciting new online product available for *IT Today.* A nominally priced token grants students access through our website to a wealth of resources—all corresponding to computer literacy. Features include an interactive glossary; current events with quizzing, assessment, and measurement options; Web survey; links to related text content; and WWW searching capability via Northern Lights, an academic search engine.

www.dushkin.com/powerweb/

TABLE OF
contents

IT Today

THE MODERN COMPUTER
THE MODERN COMPUTER
THE MODERN COMPUTER
THE MODERN COMPUTER
MODERN COMPUTER
THE MODERN COMPUTER
THE MODERN COMPUTER

learning OBJECTIVES

- What are the two types of hardware components in a PC?

- What are the four tasks or operations that hardware performs?

- What are the three types of computer software?

- What does having communications capabilities mean?

- What are the four steps in using your PC?

- What does "crossing the digital divide" mean?

- What does the computer work with to create information?

- Why is it so important that computing be safe and secure?

chapter **O N E**

REMEMBER the television show "Star Trek"? James T. Kirk, captain of the *USS Enterprise,* could not have flown his spacecraft without the help of the ship's computer. On board the *Enterprise*, the computer was more than technology—it was an essential appliance. It spoke: "Program complete, enter when ready." It always knew the ship's status: "A loss of stability resulting from the impact of a plasma charge." It was connected to a vast library of important information: "There are no recorded relationships between plasma storms and specified readings." It could even prepare meals and drinks for the crew.

WHEN "Star Trek" first aired in 1966, no computer could actually do any of this. As we embark upon the 21st century, look at the progress we've made. Ask yourself these questions: Can you talk to your PC? Is it able to tell you what it's doing? Are you able to obtain information from a wide variety of sources? Can you use a computer to order a pizza or groceries? Of course, the answer to all these questions is, as Mr. Spock would say, "Aye, aye, Captain." Computers are no longer science fiction for the few. They are everyday appliances for most of us.

WILLIAM Shatner, the actor who portrayed Captain Kirk through 79 episodes and seven *Star Trek* movies, has remained interested in the cutting edge of computer technology. He is the media spokesperson for Priceline.com, an e-commerce website that lets customers name the price they're willing to pay for airline tickets, long-distance telephone service, hotel accommodations, and groceries. "As soon as I started to see the connection priceline.com was making with its customers, I knew priceline.com's management was onto something that would fundamentally change the way people buy things for the better." Shatner is also the head of C.O.R.E. Digital Effects, a computer animation studio based in his hometown of Toronto, Ontario, that created the special effects for such movies as *Fly Away Home, Cube,* and *Walking on the Moon.*

UNDERSTANDING THE COMPUTER SYSTEM

1.1 SO YOU WANT TO BUY A PC?

When you buy a PC, just exactly what are you paying for? In most cases, you are buying hardware, software, communications capabilities, technical support, and a warranty. Understanding what you're buying is a good way to learn the four components that make up a computer system: hardware, software, communications capabilities, and you, the person who uses the computer. No matter how great the computer, it can't do a thing unless you give it instructions and data to work with.

Let's look at what you get when you buy a PC, the hardware, the software, and the communications capabilities.

Hardware. The components we physically touch are called **hardware.** These components fall into two categories. In the first category is the system unit, which is what we regard as the computer itself. The second category is the peripherals, or components that connect to the system unit. Peripherals are the components that make it possible for us to actually use the computer.

- The microprocessor is the computer itself and does all the computing. Faster microprocessors are best for games, multimedia, and programming.
- Random Access Memory (RAM) speeds processing. The more, the better.
- Storage devices keep your programs and files safe and organized—the hard disk drive is the primary storage device, CD-ROMs are used to install programs and make copies. Floppy disks and zip disks are also used to make copies, and DVD disks play videos and movies.
- Expansion cards and ports connect the system unit to peripherals.

LEARNING THE lingo

hardware The physical devices or components that make up the computer system. Hardware falls into two categories: **system unit** and **peripherals.**

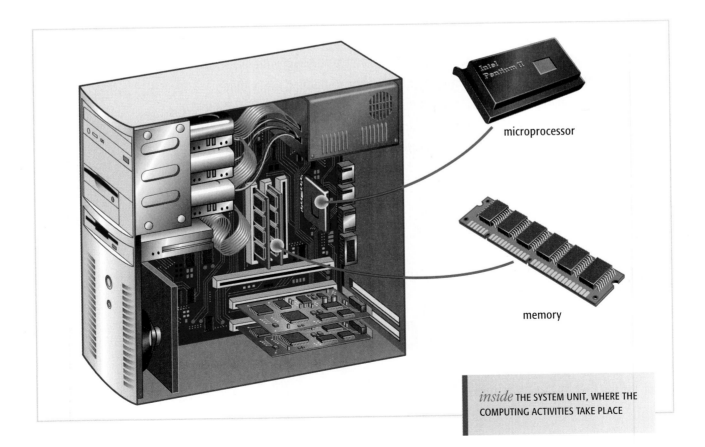

microprocessor

memory

inside THE SYSTEM UNIT, WHERE THE COMPUTING ACTIVITIES TAKE PLACE

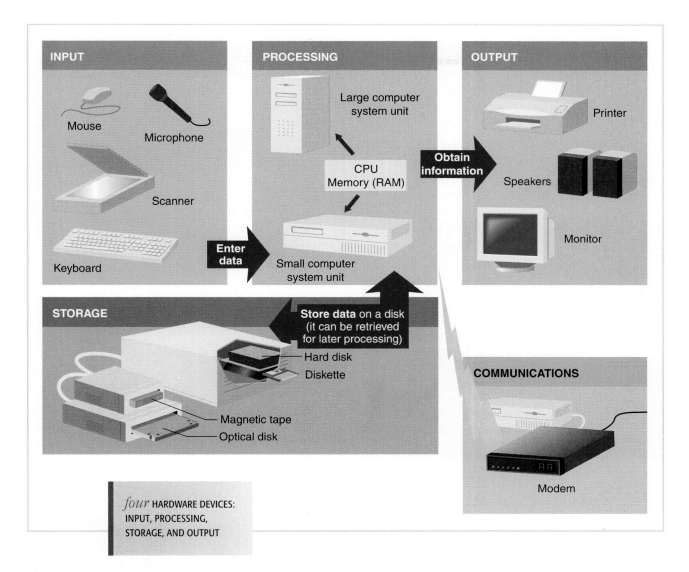

INPUT

Mouse

Microphone

Scanner

Keyboard

Enter data

PROCESSING

Large computer system unit

CPU
Memory (RAM)

Small computer system unit

Obtain information

OUTPUT

Printer

Speakers

Monitor

STORAGE

Store data on a disk (it can be retrieved for later processing)

Hard disk

Diskette

Magnetic tape

Optical disk

COMMUNICATIONS

Modem

four HARDWARE DEVICES: INPUT, PROCESSING, STORAGE, AND OUTPUT

Peripherals are components we use to work with the computer.

- The keyboard lets us enter data into the computer.
- The mouse is used to give the computer instructions.
- The video monitor lets us see the work we're doing and watch recorded video.
- Speakers let us hear computer messages and listen to recorded sound, such as music.
- The printer gives us the results of our work.

What Hardware Does. The hardware performs the computing tasks or operations. Taken together, there are four kinds of hardware devices:

- Input
- Processing
- Storage
- Output

These four devices also represent the four **computer operations** that are performed when we use a computer. We use **input** devices, such as the *keyboard* and *mouse,* to issue instructions and enter data, which is sent to the computer chip for **processing,** obviously the most important of the computer operations. The work we create is saved on a **storage** device so we can work with it again

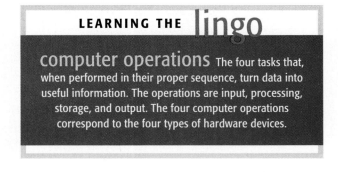

LEARNING THE lingo

computer operations The four tasks that, when performed in their proper sequence, turn data into useful information. The operations are input, processing, storage, and output. The four computer operations correspond to the four types of hardware devices.

issuing THE CLOSE COMMAND, YOU SEND AN INSTRUCTION TO THE PROCESSOR, WHICH IN TURN STORES THE FILE ON THE HARD DISK DRIVE, THEN CLOSES THE FILE.

later. Finally, we see the results of our work using **output** devices, such as the *monitor* or *printer*. Once the four operations have been accomplished, the computer has processed data into information for us to use.

Software. Even though we are usually more interested in the hardware aspects of buying a PC, the first decision is really about **software.** Almost all PCs come "bundled" with some software to help you get started. You often have

LEARNING THE

software The programs and instructions that tell the computer hardware what tasks to execute. Software falls into three basic categories: **system software** including the *operating system,* **application software** and **utility software.**

E-Notes
Better, faster, and cheaper.

PCs are constantly being improved, from the microprocessor to the DVD drive, on average about every six months. Basically, they continually get better, faster, and cost less. Most manufacturers offer system packages, so you don't have to handpick every component. Trust them; they know what they're doing. A good rule of thumb is to buy as much computer as you can afford. You can always upgrade later. And one more thing: Just because your PC is a year or two or three old doesn't mean it's obsolete. PCs have a much longer life span than the manufacturers would like you to believe.

PC & You: *WHERE AND HOW TO BUY YOUR PC*

There are many ways to buy a PC. If you prefer to walk into a store and get personal help from a salesperson, then by all means do so. You can also order a PC through a catalog, over the phone, over the Web, directly from the manufacturer, or from a discount warehouse. In most cases, you'll have your new PC in a week or less. Be sure to comparison shop, even though you may not see the exact same manufacturer and model number in a store that you see in a catalog. The safest way to buy a computer is with a major credit card, to assure that you have protection and recourse in case something happens to your order. Be sure to ask about the warranty. Can you return the computer if it breaks down within a certain period of time? How long is the warranty? Can you extend it? Even though computers usually fail within the first 90 days, extended warranties are so inexpensive that it doesn't make sense not to buy one.

CHECKLIST FOR BUYING YOUR PC

How much? Buy as much PC as you can afford.
Where? Retail, catalog, phone, online.
How? Use a major credit card. Look for secure online ordering.
Who? Always buy from a reputable, well-known company with a good warranty.

some choice in the software, but basically you're going to get an operating system and an application suite.

We work with several different types of software, some more than others.

System Software.
System software coordinates between hardware and application software. The Start menu lets you use operating system programs, such as Find. It also opens up a directory of all the software applications on your computer.

- Windows 98 and Internet Explorer are bundled together.
- You may also get Netscape Communicator as your Web browser.

Application Software.
Most new computers come with an *application suite*, sometimes called *integrated software*, which contains most of the popular applications. A major advantage of a suite is that the applications all work together harmoniously. The home-oriented package is called Microsoft Works; the business-oriented package is called Microsoft Office. Some other popular integrated applications include Quicken TurboTax Deluxe, RealPlayer, and Macromedia Dreamweaver.

- Microsoft Works 2000 offers word processing and spreadsheet capabilities, a database manager, calendar, and address book.
- Corel WordPerfect Suite and Microsoft Office 2000 are more complete application suites, offering additional applications for presentation graphics, desktop publishing, and Web page design.

Utility Software.
Helper programs are used with both system software and application software. Antivirus programs help keep your computer's data safe. Other popular utilities include screensavers, file compression, security and encryption, and hard disk maintenance.

E-Notes
Cyberspace.

"I used to think that cyberspace was 50 years away. What I thought was 50 years away, was only 10 years away. And what I thought was 10 years away. . . it was already here. I just wasn't aware of it yet."

Science fiction writer Bruce Sterling, author of *Distraction* (quoted in www.quoteland.com)

Communications Capabilities.
One of the best things about using a PC is going online to use the Internet, or going into cyberspace as some like to say. *Communications capabilities* refers to the PC's having the right hardware and software installed so that it can connect to the Internet or other online resources.

Through the PC's communications capabilities, the Internet offers three incredibly powerful resources:

- *Information resources*, vast storehouses of information on a wide variety of topics on millions of World Wide Web sites.
- *E-commerce*, or online shopping.
- *Communication* with other people using the Internet.

Information Resources.
What have you used the Internet for? The first two resources are services provided on the World Wide Web, or Web for short. The third is often called e-mail. Perhaps you've used all three.

Once it became possible for just about anyone to create a website, the Internet exploded with information. Many people who have an interest or hobby posted their knowledge, experiences, and information on the Web for all to use and share. **Search engines** have made it easier to find information resources and websites. As a result, you don't have to trudge to the library every time you need to write a research paper.

LEARNING THE lingo

search engine A website that uses software to search the World Wide Web to find other websites that contain requested information. By typing a few words into the query box, the search engine will index and identify sources of information on the subject.

e-commerce The ability of a consumer to shop for products and services from websites—placing an order, making an electronic payment (usually with a credit card), and arranging shipment—all without human intervention.

E-commerce or Online Shopping.
Buying things on the Web is called electronic commerce, or **e-commerce.** For many of us, shopping has become a simple, quick, and pleasant experience on the Web. Traditional shopping in

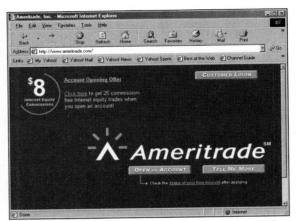

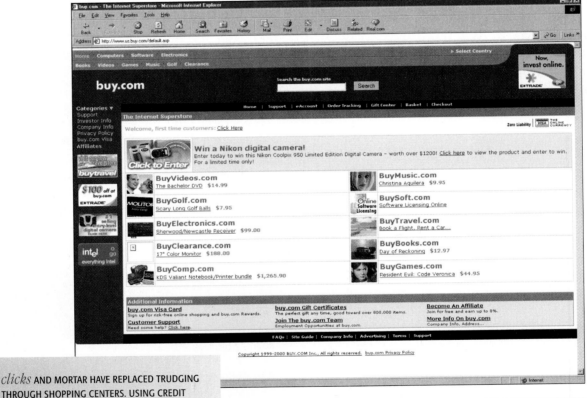

clicks AND MORTAR HAVE REPLACED TRUDGING THROUGH SHOPPING CENTERS. USING CREDIT CARDS TO MAKE ONLINE PURCHASES IS AS SAFE, IF NOT SAFER, THAN SHOPPING BY TELEPHONE.

E-Notes

The best search engines.

According to SearchEngineWatch.com, the most popular search engines are Yahoo!, MSN, Netscape, Go (Infoseek), Lycos, Excite, and AltaVista. A new search engine, Northern Light, was introduced in 1999 and won the *PC Magazine* Editor's Choice award.

what are called "bricks and mortar" stores may be fun, but it takes planning, gas, and lots of time.

For many purchases, "clicks and mortar"—electronic commerce or e-commerce—is a lot more convenient. Although not ideal for all types of shopping, the Web makes it easy to shop for the best prices and, in many cases, offers a broader selection of merchandise than you find in stores. Shipping is usually inexpensive and quick. You can shop more intelligently, more quickly, and make

once YOU'VE CHOSEN THE BEST PC FOR YOU, IT'S SIMPLE TO ORDER IT OVER THE WEB. IF YOU SELECT A PREPACKAGED SYSTEM, IT WILL BE SHIPPED TO YOU WITHIN A FEW DAYS. A CUSTOM SYSTEM MAY TAKE A WEEK OR SO.

better purchasing decisions than you can by running all over town. According to the *eMarketer Report,* the biggest product categories include:

- Computer products (hardware, software, accessories)
- Books
- Music
- Financial services
- Entertainment
- Home electronics
- Apparel
- Gifts and flowers
- Travel services
- Toys
- Tickets
- Information

Some people are reluctant to make purchases over the Web, fearing their credit card number will be stolen or misused. In fact, it is quite safe, since computers, not people, see it. Most statistics report that making a telephone credit card purchase is riskier than an e-commerce purchase.

Communication. Electronic mail, or **e-mail,** is becoming the most popular form of human communication. E-mail has also replaced many business telephone conversations, which cannot occur until both people are at their phones. Hikers in Denali Park, Alaska, stop by the Black Bear Café to use its Internet PC to send and receive e-mail messages with friends and family. Grown children buy computers for their parents so they can write each other more frequently and easily. E-mail also saves money: Since electronic documents can be sent via e-mail, expensive overnight delivery services aren't needed as often.

Although the main way we communicate with others via computer is with electronic mail, or e-mail, people sometimes like to join online chat groups where you

PC *and* You: BUYING YOUR PC ON THE WEB

The Web is a great place to buy a PC. You can get answers to your questions, look at many brands and models, and compare prices. You can select a prepackaged system or save some money by buying a refurbished computer.

Perhaps best of all, you can design, or *configure,* your own system. As the Web is visual and interactive, you can explore options and learn more about each one. If you've set a limit on how much you want to spend, you can update the system price as you add or change components.

LEARNING THE lingo

e-mail A software application that allows you to send messages to other people over the Internet. E-mail is quick and inexpensive. Messages may be typed, and files containing additional information may be attached to messages.

exchange typed messages in "real time." E-mail is becoming a more useful tool as we gain the ability to send not just typed messages but files that contain text, graphics, sound, and video—and even the ability to record spoken messages. Soon it will be commonplace to have telephone conversations over the Internet.

1.2 HOW WILL YOU USE YOUR PC?

You know that the computer system is made up of hardware, software, communications, and you. Your job is to give the computer instructions and data so that it can perform its work. A lot of this is done for you, such as loading the operating system and application software. That leaves the most interesting tasks for you to do yourself. Here is how you typically begin using your PC:

1. You sit down in front of your PC and flip on the power switch. The computer goes through a series of system checks to insure that all the hardware components are functioning. This includes the keyboard and mouse, monitor, and the chips and circuits inside the computer cabinet, called the *system unit*. The hard disk drive

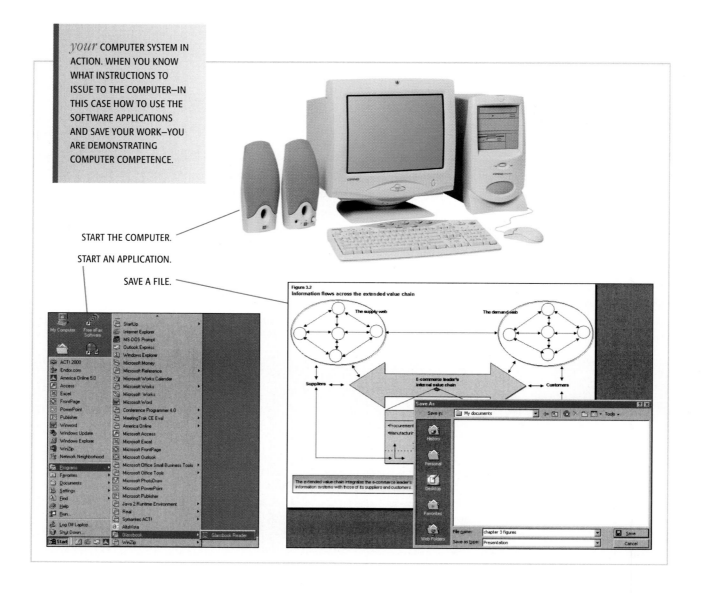

your COMPUTER SYSTEM IN ACTION. WHEN YOU KNOW WHAT INSTRUCTIONS TO ISSUE TO THE COMPUTER—IN THIS CASE HOW TO USE THE SOFTWARE APPLICATIONS AND SAVE YOUR WORK—YOU ARE DEMONSTRATING COMPUTER COMPETENCE.

START THE COMPUTER.

START AN APPLICATION.

SAVE A FILE.

the MODERN PC. NO LONGER JUST A MACHINE FOR TYPING TEXT AND CRUNCHING NUMBERS, IT IS DESIGNED FOR MANY MULTIMEDIA USES, SUCH AS SOUND AND VIDEO, AS WELL AS FOR SURFING THE WEB AND CHECKING YOUR E-MAIL.

begins spinning in order to load the software that is installed on your PC.

2. First to load is the system software, then the Windows operating system. These load automatically for you. Once they are loaded, certain utilities such as Norton AntiVirus or Dialup Networking (which you may instruct to load manually or automatically) load. Once the operating system and utilities are loaded and running, you can begin using your applications.

3. Each time you start an application (or a utility), you are issuing an instruction to your PC. Each time you perform a specific task within an application, such as naming a spreadsheet file or typing in a website address in a Web browser, you are issuing an instruction.

4. The instruction is usually issued in software — either the operating system or the application — and is completed by the hardware. For example, saving a file involves issuing an instruction to the operating system to name the file, then saving it permanently in a specified location — usually in the My Documents folder — on the hard disk drive.

Ten years ago, people mostly used the PC for word processing and spreadsheets. Today, we use a computer for so many different things it's almost an extension of our thought. Build your own website? No problem. Create a presentation for your sociology class? Ready in no time.

Add a few hundred bucks worth of SoundBlaster hardware and software and you can have a digital audio recording studio that rivals a commercial radio station. And while you're at it, have you ever wanted to direct and produce your own movies? Go for it — with your PC.

The modern PC is probably the world's best thinker-toy. Charles Lecht, the late computer guru and futurist, once said, "What the lever is to the arm, the computer is to the mind." What you can do with a computer is limited only by your imagination and the software applications available. Some are *tools* for information and knowledge management. Some are *problem solvers* that help us do things better, or even do things we couldn't without a computer. Some are *lifestyle extensions*, applications we use for fun or just because we're interested in them. Here are a few ways other people are using their PCs, which just might give you a few ideas.

The modern PC. It's a part of our lives. Once in a while you meet a few people who say they're not interested in using a computer, or who flat out say they hate computers. But read the two remarks in "Crossing the Digital Divide" (on page 16) to see what happens to people who are reluctant to embrace new technologies. The truth is, we really can't live or function in our society without computers. As these few examples point out, the modern computer is really useful. It is constantly becoming more adaptable to our needs, whereas 10 years ago it was pretty much the other way around.

build YOUR OWN WEBSITE— AND BUSINESS

Casey Fenton, 21 years old, and Django Bliss, 20, are two freelance Web designers who realized there was no effective central "office" for people like themselves to make the business world aware of their talents. In 1998, they created and launched HireAbility.com, a website where freelancers can post their qualifications and where businesses can go to find help. They designed and maintain the website themselves. "Most businesses don't realize that they can save thousands of dollars utilizing the Web, and many thousands more by outsourcing," says Django.

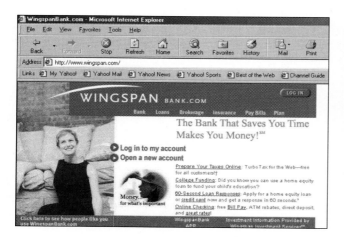

pay YOUR BILLS AND MANAGE YOUR MONEY ONLINE

If you attend college away from home or if you travel frequently, you know it can be a pain to do your banking and bill paying. That's why online banking is so cool: All you need is a Web browser and an account. The rest is almost all electronic. And if you have a money market or mutual fund, you can manage your investments online too.

using THE COMPUTER TO GET BETTER IDEAS

People have solved many interesting problems using a special application like IdeaFisher. First you use IdeaFisher's QBank, which asks you questions that help generate words and phrases. These words and phrases are then turned over to the IdeaBank, which generates new words and concepts from which make a final choice. "I've used this process to come up with a creative new product name or a solution to a problem. It provides me with countless opportunities to consider an issue from a different point of view," says Howard Fields, director of marketing for speech and pen products at IBM. Comedian Drew Carey, author of *Dirty Jokes and Beer,* says "I used a great program, IdeaFisher. . . without it, I couldn't have written this book."

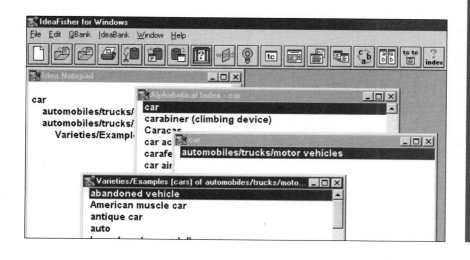

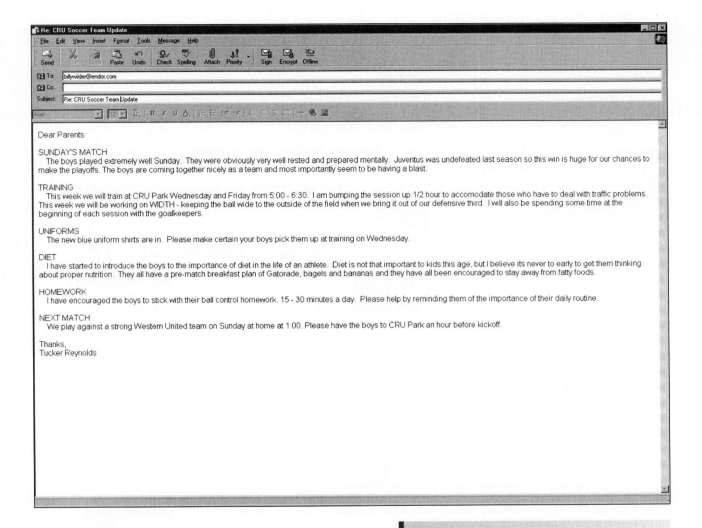

Re: CRU Soccer Team Update

To: billywilder@endor.com
Cc:
Subject: Re: CRU Soccer Team Update

Dear Parents:

SUNDAY'S MATCH
The boys played extremely well Sunday. They were obviously very well rested and prepared mentally. Juventus was undefeated last season so this win is huge for our chances to make the playoffs. The boys are coming together nicely as a team and most importantly seem to be having a blast.

TRAINING
This week we will train at CRU Park Wednesday and Friday from 5:00 - 6:30. I am bumping the session up 1/2 hour to accomodate those who have to deal with traffic problems. This week we will be working on WIDTH - keeping the ball wide to the outside of the field when we bring it out of our defensive third. I will also be spending some time at the beginning of each session with the goalkeepers.

UNIFORMS
The new blue uniform shirts are in. Please make certain your boys pick them up at training on Wednesday.

DIET
I have started to introduce the boys to the importance of diet in the life of an athlete. Diet is not that important to kids this age, but I believe its never to early to get them thinking about proper nutrition. They all have a pre-match breakfast plan of Gatorade, bagels and bananas and they have all been encouraged to stay away from fatty foods.

HOMEWORK
I have encouraged the boys to stick with their ball control homework. 15 - 30 minutes a day. Please help by reminding them of the importance of their daily routine.

NEXT MATCH
We play against a strong Western United team on Sunday at home at 1:00. Please have the boys to CRU Park an hour before kickoff.

Thanks,
Tucker Reynolds

using E-MAIL TO IMPROVE COMMUNICATION

The Medway, Massachusetts, Jazz soccer team has 15 members. "Before e-mail," says coach Tucker Reynolds, "this type of weekly communication was unlikely. Notices would have to be typed, printed, copied, folded, slapped with address labels, stamped and mailed. There is no way this information could be telephoned to all of the parents."

using HIGH-TECH TOOLS TO CREATE HIGH-TECH DESIGNS

Michael Jager's design firm, Jager Di Paola Kemp, created the trademark motion designs for Burton snowboards. Average age of JDK's designers is 27. It's all done on PCs using Adobe Illustrator and PhotoShop applications. "In order to create a brand identity that has meaning and energy," says Jager, "you have to ask 'How can we be relevant and also break down what exists now; what can we shift and change'?"

learning HOW TO UPGRADE YOUR PC

Private John Booth bought his PC from the Gateway website and uses it primarily as a learning tool. Taking online courses from his Army barracks room, he was able to land the job as battalion computer guru. Recently, he's been studying some material on Cnet.com to learn more about multimedia and creating simulations on his PC. Then he reads the software and hardware reviews on the *PC World* and *Computer Shopper* websites to get the best prices on what he intends to buy.

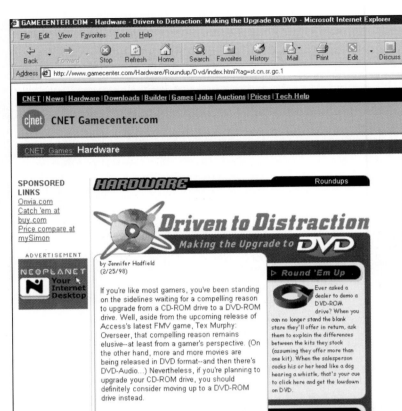

using THE WEB TO KEEP UP WITH YOUR FAVORITE TEAM

Everybody has favorite sports or teams, but you won't necessarily find the coverage you want, when you want it, in the newspaper. That's only one reason Yahoo! Sports is so valuable.

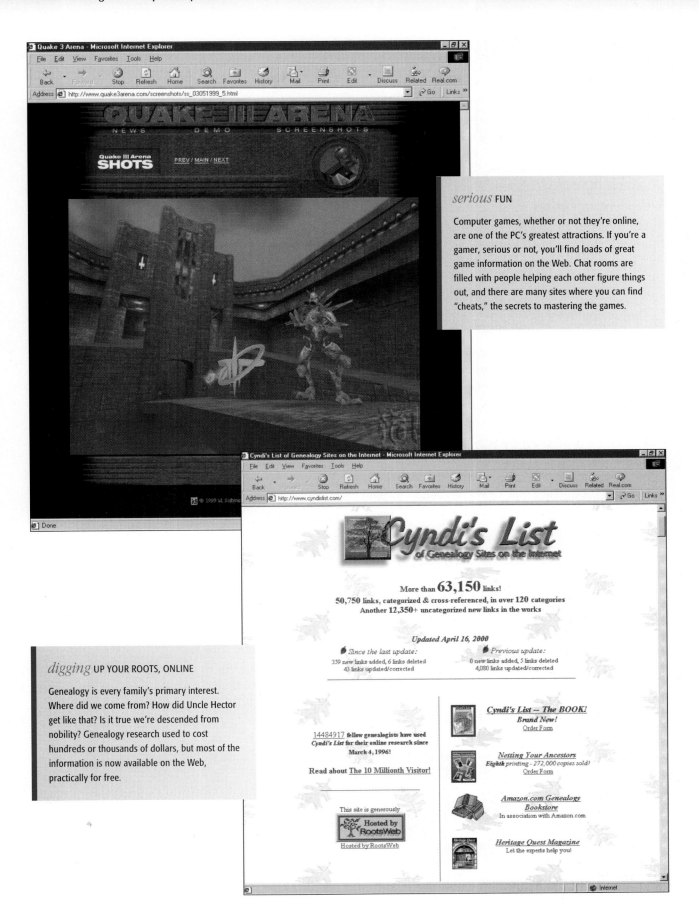

serious FUN

Computer games, whether or not they're online, are one of the PC's greatest attractions. If you're a gamer, serious or not, you'll find loads of great game information on the Web. Chat rooms are filled with people helping each other figure things out, and there are many sites where you can find "cheats," the secrets to mastering the games.

digging UP YOUR ROOTS, ONLINE

Genealogy is every family's primary interest. Where did we come from? How did Uncle Hector get like that? Is it true we're descended from nobility? Genealogy research used to cost hundreds or thousands of dollars, but most of the information is now available on the Web, practically for free.

1.3 CROSSING THE DIGITAL DIVIDE

Have you ever said something that you later wish you hadn't? Many prominent people have made predictions about technology that they'd like to take back. Here are two opinions made by the heads of computer companies:

- In 1953, Thomas J. Watson, Sr., chairman of the board of IBM, said "I think there is a world market for about five computers."

- In 1977, Kenneth Olsen, president of Digital Equipment Corporation, told the World Future Society that "There is no reason for any individual to have a computer in their home."

How our attitudes toward computers have changed! Most of us need to cross the *digital divide* at some point. Crossing the digital divide means understanding how the computer helps make each of us more competent in using the computer in our daily lives. Whether it's homework, shopping on the Web, preparing our tax return, or performing our daily work, we can do more, and do it better, than we could without a computer. It's the ongoing adventure of learning new ways to make the computer more useful—the lever of the mind, as Charles Lecht suggested.

Crossing the digital divide means becoming computer-savvy—knowing how to use your PC to get things done. Here are some examples:

- You can write a term paper and edit it three or more times on the computer screen before you print it. Think of how long that would take if you had to edit it by hand and then retype it each time on a typewriter.

- You can arrange a meeting or get a bunch of friends together more efficiently by sending them an e-mail message than you can by trying to call them. You write one message and send it once, instead of calling and leaving messages for each person.

- You can learn about a new pop group by reading reviews on the Web and listening to sound clips on your computer's speakers. You can also make your own custom CDs or download music to an MP3 music player. This means you get the music you want without having to drive to the mall,

and you get to hear it and even select exactly what you want, often for free.

- You're planning a cross-country bicycling trip. Using a mapping and trip planning software application, you plot the entire route, including daily mileages so you can determine the location of campgrounds or motels where you'll need reservations, which you make online at various websites. Once you're finished, you print out the maps, itineraries, and reservations. You've not only saved time and money but you've integrated the three activities in a way you never could without a computer.

What do you want to do with your PC? Write down two or three things you do, or would like to do, with your computer and e-mail your list to us. We'll post the most interesting stories on this book's website for you and your fellow students to read. Reach us at ittoday@ mcgraw-hill.com

1.4 HOW DO YOU WORK WITH INFORMATION?

We live in the Information Age, so of course everybody is always looking for information. It might be a movie review, a phone number, the price of the new Smashing Pumpkins CD, or the biography of Leonardo da Vinci. Computers are really good at working with information. The computer takes the **data** you give it and turns it into useful **information** that you can use for all kinds of things.

The computer is also changing the way people work, and even work itself. If you can use a computer and work with information, you're going to have really great jobs for the rest of your life.

How do you work with information? Think about it, and then make a short list of your most important kinds of information, how you use or would use the PC to work with it, and how the PC makes it better or easier to do so.

Information I use	How the PC works with it	How the PC improves it

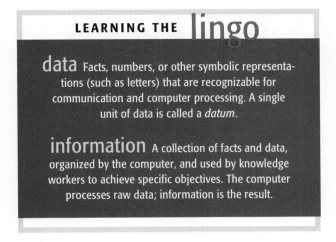

LEARNING THE lingo

data Facts, numbers, or other symbolic representations (such as letters) that are recognizable for communication and computer processing. A single unit of data is called a *datum*.

information A collection of facts and data, organized by the computer, and used by knowledge workers to achieve specific objectives. The computer processes raw data; information is the result.

E-Notes
On-screen cues.

The window at the far right side of the Start menu bar displays many of the active utilities. If you roll your mouse pointer over each icon and hold it a second, you'll get a message describing the utility. If you're online and would like to know the speed at which you're connected to the Internet, double-click on the twin blinking green computer screens icon.

Information tells you something you didn't know or that you need to know. Information is most meaningful when it is applied to a specific situation or used for solving a specific problem. These screens shown here and on the next page are some examples.

One of the most interesting things about information is that we are able to get it and use it on many new and different kinds of *information appliances*. Steve Ballmer, president of Microsoft, says, "Whether it's shopping, sharing information like your calendar or your family website, or online applications and support for businesses of all sizes, these new services will be enabled across an entire new range of devices (such as cellular phones and personal digital assistants), giving users access to their information from any place, on any device." (*Wired*, January 2000, p. 84)

information MAY BE IN THE FORM OF BUSINESS FACTS AND FIGURES, NEWSPAPERS OR BOOKS, SOUND OR VIDEO, OR CREATING THE SOFTWARE TOOLS AND ENTERTAINMENT MEDIA OF THE FUTURE. THE INFORMATION YOU CREATE, READ, OR PRINT IS SAVED IN A FILE ON ONE OF THE COMPUTER'S STORAGE DEVICES. HOW MANY DIFFERENT TYPES OF INFORMATION CAN YOU IDENTIFY ON THIS WEBSITE?

this PROJECT MANAGEMENT SOFTWARE APPLICATION IS CONCERNED WITH PLANNING. IT CAPTURES DATA ABOUT THE STEPS INVOLVED IN PREPARING A NEW MERCHANDISE CATALOG, AS WELL AS THE ROLES AND RESPONSIBILITIES OF EACH PERSON IN THE PROCESS.

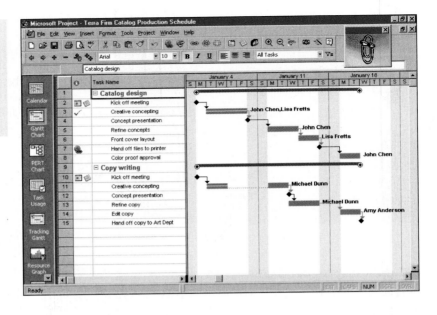

this WEB SEARCH ENGINE TAKES THE DATA YOU TYPE—IN THIS CASE, THREE WORDS—AND PROVIDES A WIDE VARIETY OF INFORMATION ABOUT THE SUBJECT. NOTE THE CUSTOM SEARCH FOLDERS ON THE LEFT.

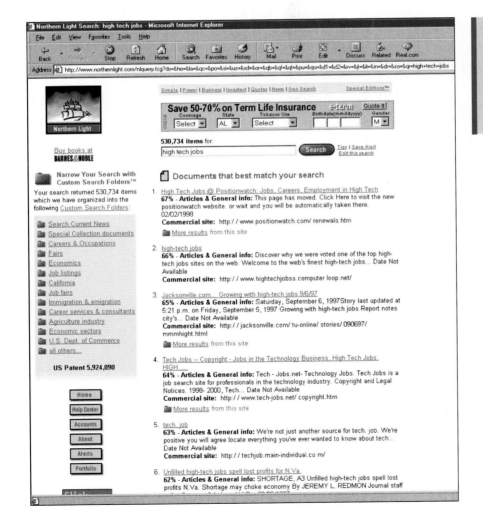

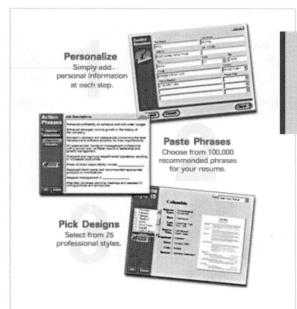

Personalize
Simply add
personal information
at each step.

Paste Phrases
Choose from 100,000
recommended phrases
for your resume.

Pick Designs
Select from 25
professional styles.

the PROGRAM HELPS YOU CREATE YOUR OWN RÉSUMÉ ON PAPER OR IN DIGITAL FORMAT FOR POSTING TO A WEBSITE. YOU TYPE IN YOUR PERSONAL DATA AND THE APPLICATION TURNS IT INTO INFORMATION IN THE FORM OF A RÉSUMÉ.

talking*issues*

SAFE, SECURE COMPUTING

"Hey! Somebody got into my computer!" Nobody wants their computer broken into, but the fact is, it happens all the time. It might be harmless—like the guy who left his PC on in his office, so the cleaning crew used it to play games. It might be someone stealing files from your computer. It might be a virus attack. It might be a system crash. Some of the things you can do to make sure your computer is secure include:

▶▶ When you're through using your computer, always close Windows and turn the power off correctly. You close Windows by clicking Start, Shut Down.

▶▶ Use a password if you're worried about prying eyes. The Windows password is easily compromised, so find a utility program that has one, such as a screen saver.

▶▶ Use an antivirus program and always scan files people send you on e-mail.

▶▶ Don't eat, drink, or smoke near your computer.

▶▶ Perform regular maintenance on your PC, such as backing up and defragging your hard drive.

▶▶ When you remove or uninstall a program, use Windows or the program's uninstall utility to do so. Don't just delete it or your computer might not run right.

WHO OWNS INFORMATION?

As we enter into the full-blown age of information, this is the question we need to ask ourselves all the time. Indeed, one of the responsibilities we have as computer-literate people is to recognize information ownership and areas involving copyright. Every time you think about using information from a website, you should be checking to see if it is copyrighted. If it is, you need permission to use it.

There are three primary areas of information ownership and copyright: personal, business, and external:

▶▶ *Personal.* You have the copyright and intellectual ownership to anything you write or create, without having to legally or formally register such ownership.

▶▶ *Business.* Generally, your employer owns all forms of information you create while on the job, whether it is a document or even the invention of a product or service.

▶▶ *External.* You are responsible for acknowledging and obtaining permission to use any information you obtain that was created and/or published by others, whether printed, copied, or electronically stored in an information retrieval system (such as a computer or on the Internet).

Violation of someone else's copyright can be a serious matter. The U.S. Copyright Law of 1978 protects your original work for 50 years when you put Copyright © followed by your name and the date. The Copyright Law provides for stiff penalties in the case of copyright violation and plagiarism. Above all, remember that copyright applies to your own unique and individual expression in writing, while neither facts nor ideas can be copyrighted. Put another way, *data* cannot be copyrighted, but *information,* which is the product of the human mind bringing ideas and interpretation to data, can be copyrighted.

chapter REVIEW

DO-IT-YOURSELF SUMMARY

1. When you buy a PC, you are buying _____, _____, communications capabilities, technical support, and a warranty.

2. The two types of hardware components in a PC are the _____ _____ and _____.

3. The most important computer operation is _____.

4. Instructions are commonly issued to the computer by using _____.

5. The software we use most of the time to do our work is called _____ software.

6. Going online means using the computer's _____ capabilities.

7. A useful tool for finding information on the Web is the _____ _____.

8. Using your computer to work with information means giving it _____ and _____.

9. _____ can be copyrighted, but ____ or _____ cannot.

KEY TERMS REVIEW

a. computer operations
b. data
c. e-commerce
d. e-mail
e. hardware
f. information
g. search engine
h. software

___ **1.** The physical devices that make up a computer.

___ **2.** They are the same as the four kinds of hardware devices.

___ **3.** Used to give computers instructions.

___ **4.** A tool for locating information on the Web.

___ **5.** Conducting business over the Internet.

___ **6.** A message sent over the Internet.

___ **7.** What is fed into the computer for processing.

___ **8.** The results of computer operations.

KEY CONCEPTS REVIEW

a. application software

b. communications capabilities

c. peripherals

d. system software

e. system unit

f. utility software

____ **1.** The cabinet that houses the computer itself.

____ **2.** Hardware devices that allow a person to use the computer.

____ **3.** Starts up the computer automatically.

____ **4.** Used by people to perform work and various tasks.

____ **5.** Helpful programs used by both types of software.

____ **6.** The hardware and software needed to go online.

ANSWERS: 1. e; 2. c; 3. d; 4. a; 5. f; 6. b.

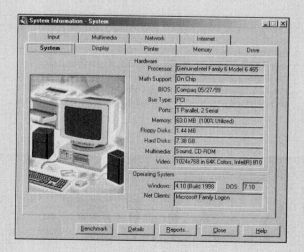

HANDS-ON EXERCISES

1. *Describe your PC.* Whether you own a PC or are using one in a lab, describe it, based on what you have learned in this chapter:

Hardware:

System unit brand name:

Input devices:

Output devices:

Software:

Operating System:

Applications (click on the Start button and look in Programs):

2. *What's inside your PC?* Most people are interested in knowing some technical details about their PC. What kind of microprocessor does yours have? How much memory? You can learn about your PC by using utilities that are part of the Windows operating system.

Click on the My Computer icon, then right-click on the computer icon at the top left to go to the menu. Select System Information to see your system specifications. You'll see a screen like the one shown to the left.

Write down the following information about your PC:

My computer has:

1. The _____ processor

2. _____ MB of Memory (click on Memory)

3. _____ floppy disk drive

4. _____ CD-ROM drive

5. _____ DVD drive

6. A hard disk drive with _____ of storage space (click on Drive)

7. _____ operating system

8. My Internet connection speed is _____

learning
OBJECTIVES

- What is the relationship between the World Wide Web and the Internet?

- How do you find a website?

- How do you get from one website to another?

- What are the different types of websites?

- How is information organized on different types of websites?

- What software application is used to browse the Web?

- What is another widely used Internet application?

- What constitutes good manners when using computers?

chapter **TWO**

TIM is the director of the World Wide Web Consortium (W3C) at MIT's Laboratory for Computer Science. In 1999, he won the coveted John D. and Catherine T. MacArthur Foundation "genius" Fellowship. He is author of *Weaving the Web: The Original Design and Ultimate Destiny of the World Wide Web* by its Inventor (San Francisco:Harper, 1999).

CAN you imagine coming up with the idea to create the World Wide Web? That's exactly what Tim Berners-Lee did. But "there was no 'Eureka!' moment," he explains in his book, *Weaving the Web*. "Inventing the World Wide Web involved my growing realization that there was a power in arranging ideas in an unconstrained, weblike way."

TIM got the idea for the Web from a one hundred-year-old book. "When I first began tinkering with a software program that eventually gave rise to the idea of the World Wide Web, I named it Enquire, short for *Enquire Within upon Everything*, a musty old book of Victorian advice I noticed as a child in my parents' house outside London. With its title suggestive of magic, the book served as a portal to a world of information, everything from how to remove clothing stains to tips on investing money. Not a perfect analogy for the Web, but a primitive starting point.

"*WHAT* that first bit of Enquire code led me to was something much larger, a vision encompassing the decentralized, organic growth of ideas, technology, and society. The vision I have for the Web is about anything being potentially connected with anything. It is a vision that provides us with new freedom, and allows us to grow faster than we ever could [before]."

TIM'S idea for the Web was to make computers work with information in new ways. "A computer typically keeps information in rigid hierarchies and matrices, whereas the human mind has the special ability to link random bits of data. When I smell coffee, strong and stale, I may find myself again in a small room over a corner coffeehouse in Oxford. My brain makes a link, and instantly transports me there…the idea stayed with me that computers could become much more powerful if they could be programmed to link otherwise unconnected information."

AND that's how the World Wide Web came to be.

USING THE INTERNET

2

2.1 WHAT IS THE INTERNET?

In Chapter 1 we learned that the computer system is made up of hardware, software, communications capabilities, and you, the person who uses the computer. Now, as we begin learning about the Internet, those communications capabilities become really important. The **Internet** is a computer system too—a very large one, with hundreds of thousands of individual computer systems connected together by telephone lines and other network connections. There are more things to do and see and use and play with on the Internet than you could ever get to in a lifetime.

LEARNING THE lingo

Internet A global network of linked computers, providing many information services such as e-mail, file transfers, access to stored information, access to software programs, newsgroups, and multimedia resources.

When you and your PC are connected to the Internet, your computer system becomes part of the Internet computer system. The Internet computer system is a **network.** It gives you access to a great many online services and activities, all available from a single resource. All you need to do to use this resource is connect to the network.

Why Use a Network? It's pretty difficult *not* to use computer networks these days. Every time you use an ATM, a credit card, or voice mail, you're using a computer network. Networks make computers more useful by helping us to obtain more or better information and to work and live more productively.

Think about how handy the Internet is in these two examples:

- *Research*. Your library might have a few books you need for learning about Shakespeare, but not the movie review that appeared in *The New York Times*.

LEARNING THE lingo

network Two or more computers connected, making it possible to share computer resources and information. The Internet is the biggest computer network on earth.

"By 2010, the appearance of a new communications infrastructure is as common as the installation of new street signs in the 1990s; a morning overflight of AT&T choppers, a haze of tiny parachutes, devices landing everywhere . . . [They] perch on street lamps and curbs and customers' roofs. An hour or two passes. The system initializes, establishes power feeds, and registers mobile customers; infrared laser communication is aligned on fixed consumer endpoints. Around lunchtime, a few AT&T technicians sweep up the network poop. By evening, a year's worth of 20th-century work has been done. And it can be done again when British Telecom comes up with a better deal."

Vernor Vinge, "The Digital GAIA," Wired, January 2000, p. 76.

You can obtain a copy instantly from the *Times* website. Result: You've obtained information you would not have had access to otherwise.

- *Shopping*. You need a new software application, but the nearest retail software store is an hour away. You can visit a website, order it, and have it delivered the next day—sometimes without extra charge. You've saved time and perhaps money as well.

The Internet is actually a network of networks, all interconnected to each other. Thousands of computers are connected in these networks. Stored on these computers are software applications, games, chat rooms, and discussion groups. There's tons of information on just about anything you're interested in and stuff you can buy. Think of the Internet as one big computer, much like your own PC, but with much more to do. Here are some of the things you can use the Internet for:

- Sending and receiving files
- News and information
- Obtaining software applications for trial or short-term use
- Communicating with other people in online chat rooms
- Listening to or viewing multimedia sound or video
- Buying and selling goods and services

2.2 WHAT IS THE WORLD WIDE WEB?

The **World Wide Web** is the way most of us use the Internet's information services and resources. That's because the Web's colorful, graphical display makes it so easy. The Web is made up of thousands of networked computer systems connected to the Internet. Individuals

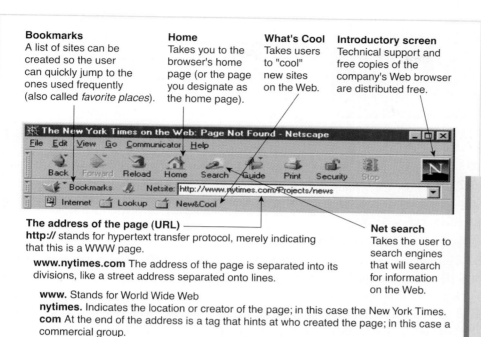

Bookmarks
A list of sites can be created so the user can quickly jump to the ones used frequently (also called *favorite places*).

Home
Takes you to the browser's home page (or the page you designate as the home page).

What's Cool
Takes users to "cool" new sites on the Web.

Introductory screen
Technical support and free copies of the company's Web browser are distributed free.

The address of the page (URL)
http:// stands for hypertext transfer protocol, merely indicating that this is a WWW page.

> **www.nytimes.com** The address of the page is separated into its divisions, like a street address separated onto lines.
>
> > **www.** Stands for World Wide Web
> > **nytimes.** Indicates the location or creator of the page; in this case the New York Times.
> > **com** At the end of the address is a tag that hints at who created the page; in this case a commercial group.
>
> **/Projects/news/** Slashes divide the names of pages that are the path to that site.

Net search
Takes the user to search engines that will search for information on the Web.

the WEB MAKES THE INTERNET EASY TO USE IN TWO WAYS. FIRST OF ALL, THE COLORS AND GRAPHICS MAKE INFORMATION EASY TO VIEW. THEN ISSUING INSTRUCTIONS IS SIMPLE: EITHER TYPE IN THE URL OR CLICK ON A HYPERTEXT LINK TO GO TO ADDITIONAL PAGES AND INFORMATION.

LEARNING THE *lingo*

World Wide Web A graphical, multimedia online information resource of networked computers, available over the Internet, with its own user interface, instructions, and means of accessing and presenting information.

like you and me, businesses, nonprofit organizations, government agencies, and others contribute to making the Web a unique place to learn about something you're interested in, download a great new game, read movie reviews, listen to your favorite music, send electronic greeting cards, and lots more.

How Web Computers Are Linked. Web computers use a means of communicating called *HyperText Transfer Protocol*, or *HTTP*, which helps identify them as World Wide

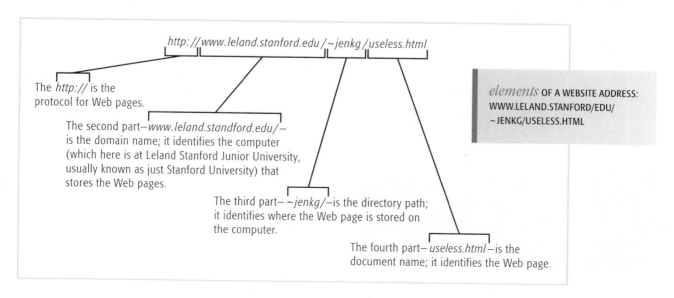

http://www.leland.stanford.edu/~jenkg/useless.html

The *http://* is the protocol for Web pages.

The second part—*www.leland.standford.edu/*—is the domain name; it identifies the computer (which here is at Leland Stanford Junior University, usually known as just Stanford University) that stores the Web pages.

The third part—*~jenkg/*—is the directory path; it identifies where the Web page is stored on the computer.

The fourth part—*useless.html*—is the document name; it identifies the Web page.

elements OF A WEBSITE ADDRESS:
WWW.LELAND.STANFORD/EDU/
~JENKG/USELESS.HTML

Web sites with files and resources we can access. Website addresses begin with the **http://** command, although we usually don't have to type it in any longer.

Computer Addresses. Each computer on the Web has a unique identification, or address, just as you have for receiving mail or phone calls. This address is called a **URL,** which stands for **Uniform Resource Locator.** You must know the URL in order to find the computer, and it must be typed in exactly, with all punctuation. An example of a complete website address is <u>http://www.mhhe.com</u>.

E-Notes
Typing URLs.

Web addresses are not case sensitive, so it doesn't matter if you type them in uppercase or lowercase. However, you must use the correct punctuation!

Finding a Website. In addition to the prefix http://, there are three elements to the website address. They are the domain name, the directory path, and the document name.

Web Designations. When we type **www.,** we are indicating we want access to World Wide Web computers. In some cases this might be slightly different, such as **www2,** but it's all the Web.

Finding a Web Computer. The Web uses something called the **domain name system,** or **DNS,** to identify the name of the computer and the type of site we want to use.

In the figure on page 25, the computer's *domain name* is leland.stanford, standing for Leland Stanford University. Most websites try to use a domain name that reflects the company or organization's name, one that stands for the name of the site, or something that logically reminds you of the site. Here are some examples:

- <u>www.buy.com</u> for shopping
- <u>www.ups.com</u> for United Parcel Service
- <u>www.wired.com</u> for the magazine *Wired*
- <u>www.playstation.com</u> for the Sony Playstation computer game system

What Type Of Website Is It? There is one more thing we must type in to finish the domain name. It is referred to as the *domain identifier.* In this case, the Leland Stanford University site is an education site, that uses the suffix **.edu** to identify it: <u>www.leland.stanford.edu</u>.

You may have noticed that a URL is similar to a filename and its extension. That's because the instructions or procedures for looking into a computer's files are essentially the same, whether on your own PC or on a computer connected in a network.

Some Common Website Domains

.edu for education: Stanford University is www.stanford.edu

.com for commercial or business: www.eTrade.com

.net also commercial or Internet-related: www.internic.net

.gov for the U.S. government: The President of the United States is www.whitehouse.gov

.org for nonprofit organizations: National Public Radio is www.npr.org

.mil for military identification: www.defenselink.mil

.ca for Canadian websites: www.aircanada.ca

.uk for United Kingdom (Great Britain) websites: www.london-calling.co.uk/

Hyperlinks. As you learned in Chapter 1, the Windows operating system makes it easy to issue instructions to the computer — simply by clicking on menus and icons. The same is true of the Web. Without the Web's graphical display, we would all be typing in arcane instructions in computerese, such as this:

info/kevdb?OTMPL=%2Fres%2Fr1.html&QFM=N&QK=5&XNavigation=&QN

One of the coolest things to click on when you're visiting a website is a hyperlink. The domain name gets you into the computer and to the website home page. From there, you may decide to browse other pages or jump to an entirely different website. You do this by clicking on a **hyperlink.**

By clicking the mouse on the hyperlink, you'll be taken directly to that page or file. A specific page on a site is separated from the site address by a / slash mark. Once you click on it, you'll see the page name appear in the URL. Here is an example of a hyperlink on the same website: www.mhhe.com/ittoday.

Hyperlinked pages contain additional information or resources, which may be stored on that computer or on any other computer on the Internet. These pages are

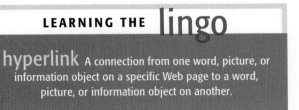

LEARNING THE lingo

hyperlink A connection from one word, picture, or information object on a specific Web page to a word, picture, or information object on another.

easy TO SPOT, A HYPERLINK IS DISPLAYED EITHER AS:

- TEXT, IDENTIFIED BY ITS COLOR (USUALLY BLUE) AND BY BEING UNDERLINED, OR

- AN IMAGE OR ICON, IDENTIFIED BY THE APPEARANCE OF A HAND, WHICH REPLACES THE ARROW WHEN THE CURSOR MOVES OVER IT.

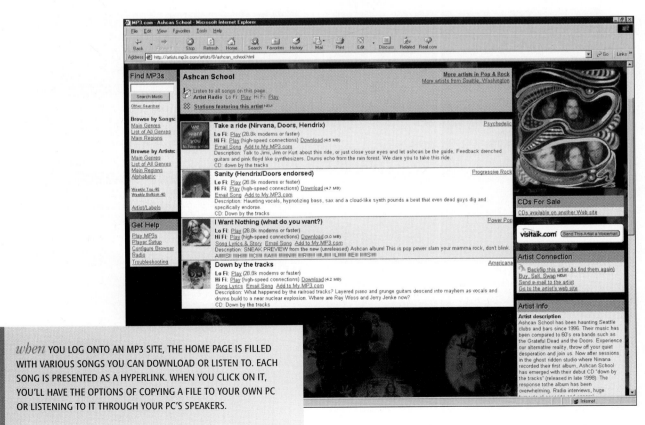

when YOU LOG ONTO AN MP3 SITE, THE HOME PAGE IS FILLED WITH VARIOUS SONGS YOU CAN DOWNLOAD OR LISTEN TO. EACH SONG IS PRESENTED AS A HYPERLINK. WHEN YOU CLICK ON IT, YOU'LL HAVE THE OPTIONS OF COPYING A FILE TO YOUR OWN PC OR LISTENING TO IT THROUGH YOUR PC'S SPEAKERS.

actually files that have been created as Web pages using a Web authoring application. The authoring application creates Web pages the same way that you would create files and pages in desktop publishing or presentation graphics or any other application. What's different is that we "turn" to those "pages" using hyperlinks.

2.3 UNDERSTANDING WEBSITES

The way you use the Web depends on what information or services you want to obtain. Do you need to find out where Custer made his last stand? Are you looking for a

The Information Quest: It's What the Internet Is All About

Website	Caption/Title
www.bigyellow.com	Find a phone number or address
www.corbis.com	Select photographs
www.broadcast.com	Listen to music and radio stations
www.cnet.com	Computer software and hardware reviews
www.sports.yahoo.com	Latest sports news
www.lowestfare.com	Discount airline tickets
www.startrekcontinuum.com	Official Star Trek site

Web SEARCH ENGINES: NO TWO ARE ALIKE

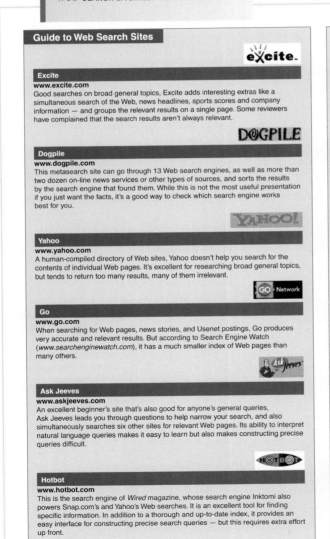

Guide to Web Search Sites

excite.

Excite
www.excite.com
Good searches on broad general topics, Excite adds interesting extras like a simultaneous search of the Web, news headlines, sports scores and company information — and groups the relevant results on a single page. Some reviewers have complained that the search results aren't always relevant.

DOGPILE

Dogpile
www.dogpile.com
This metasearch site can go through 13 Web search engines, as well as more than two dozen on-line news services or other types of sources, and sorts the results by the search engine that found them. While this is not the most useful presentation if you just want the facts, it's a good way to check which search engine works best for you.

YAHOO!

Yahoo
www.yahoo.com
A human-compiled directory of Web sites, Yahoo doesn't help you search for the contents of individual Web pages. It's excellent for researching broad general topics, but tends to return too many results, many of them irrelevant.

GO Network

Go
www.go.com
When searching for Web pages, news stories, and Usenet postings, Go produces very accurate and relevant results. But according to Search Engine Watch (*www.searchenginewatch.com*), it has a much smaller index of Web pages than many others.

Ask Jeeves

Ask Jeeves
www.askjeeves.com
An excellent beginner's site that's also good for anyone's general queries, Ask Jeeves leads you through questions to help narrow your search, and also simultaneously searches six other sites for relevant Web pages. Its ability to interpret natural language queries makes it easy to learn but also makes constructing precise queries difficult.

HOTBOT

Hotbot
www.hotbot.com
This is the search engine of *Wired* magazine, whose search engine Inktomi also powers Snap.com's and Yahoo's Web searches. It is an excellent tool for finding specific information. In addition to a thorough and up-to-date index, it provides an easy interface for constructing precise search queries — but this requires extra effort up front.

LYCOS

Lycos
www.lycos.com
Lycos provides a good selection of advanced search capabilities, like the ability to search for specific media types (JPEG files, Java scripts, and so on). Its advanced search, Lycos Pro, provides even more options. But general Web searches can produce checkered results. Also, Lycos's index of Web pages is small.

Northern Light
www.nlsearch.com
In addition to its index of Web pages, Northern Light searches through pay-per-view articles from periodicals not generally available on the Web. It sorts its results into topic headings, which can prove very useful.

AltaVista™

Alta Vista
www.altavista.net
Another excellent tool for exhaustive and precise searches, Alta Vista makes it harder than Hotbot does for beginners to construct precise queries but, once you've mastered its search syntax, it's quick and easy to use. Its results, however, can include many duplicates. Alta Vista also includes a powerful photo finder (you can search more than 11 million images): *http://image.altavista.com/cgi-bin/avncgi*

metacrawler

Metacrawler
www.metacrawler.com
This is a metasearch site, simultaneously searching Yahoo, Excite, and five other search engines, then aggregating the results. It's excellent for getting a quick hit of what's out there. But if you don't see what you want in the results, its limited search options make it tough to issue really precise queries.

iSleuth.com
Over 3,000 Searchable Databases

Internet Sleuth
www.isleuth.com
Internet Sleuth is a 3000-strong collection of specialized online databases, which can also simultaneously search up to six other search sites for Web pages, news, and other types of information. It's excellent for highly specialized searches in any subjects in its detailed directory — but the metasearch results aren't sorted intuitively.

DIRECT HIT

Direct Hit
www.directhit.com
Search engine spitting back too many results? Try Direct Hit at *www.directhit.com*, which takes your search term, polls major search engines, and show the 10 most popular sites.

summer job at a nearby high-tech company? Maybe you just want the ski conditions for the weekend. In some cases, you'll already know the URL for the website you want to use. Sometimes you can guess at the name of the site: Try typing it in and see if you hit it.

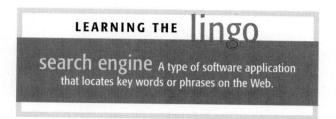

LEARNING THE lingo

search engine A type of software application that locates key words or phrases on the Web.

E-Notes
Hot Picks.

Want to find some interesting sites? There are many guides to, and awards for, the best websites. Here are a few:

- USA Today's Hot Sites: www.usatoday.com/life/cyber/ch.htm

- Go2Net's Hot 100: www.100hot.com/index.html

- Netscape's What's Cool: http://home.netscape.com/netcenter/cool.html

- Nick's Picks—a directory of cool sites: www.coolcentral.com/picks/

In addition to knowing the domain name for the website, you'll also need to know its domain identifier, mentioned earlier. For example, if you want to go to the Dell Computer website, you type **www.dell.com** since it is a business and a commercial site.

But what if you're looking for the Association of Students Preparing for a Career in Information Technology. It's unlikely the entire name of the organization will be spelled out, and it may be a commercial (.com) or a nonprofit (.org) organization. How do you find it? Well, there are two easy ways to find websites when you don't know the address. One is using a search engine and the other is using a portal.

Using Search Engines. Some websites, such as AltaVista and Northern Light, are **search engines** for you to locate other sites or specific information. However, specific websites also may have a built-in search engine feature that helps you find information on that particular site.

In addition to massive Web search engines described at the bottom of page 28, there are two other major types of search engines. The first type of search engine is the *subject search engine,* which lets you search the Web for a particular topic of interest. Some examples include gardening, energy, investing, health, law, music, regions of the country and the world, Shakespeare, and so forth. Often you can find a subject search engine site by simply typing the subject as part of the URL, for everything from www.snowboards.com to www.garden.com.

The second type of search engine is the *site-specific search engine.* This is search engine software installed on a specific website that enables you to search for information stored only on that particular website. The figure for Reel.com shows an example.

this SITE'S SEARCH ENGINE ALLOWS YOU TO SEARCH FOR MOVIES BY NAME AND CATEGORY

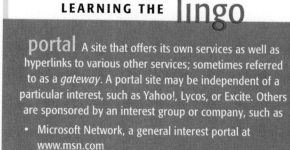

LEARNING THE lingo

portal A site that offers its own services as well as hyperlinks to various other services; sometimes referred to as a *gateway.* A portal site may be independent of a particular interest, such as Yahoo!, Lycos, or Excite. Others are sponsored by an interest group or company, such as

- Microsoft Network, a general interest portal at www.msn.com
- CNet, a computer interest portal at www.cnet.com
- Hieros Gamos, the law and government portal at www.hg.org

Portals often offer access to news, weather, e-mail, stock quotes, e-mail greeting cards, phone directories, maps and directions, shopping guides, and chat rooms or personals.

using A SEARCH ENGINE TO FIND KEYWORDS, THIS WEBSITE'S SEARCH ENGINE NOT ONLY LOCATES THE KEYWORDS YOU TYPE IN, BUT OFFERS TO SHOW YOU THE TOP 10 MOST VISITED PAGES ON ITS SITE

Using Portals. A growing number of websites have been modeled on Yahoo!, the first portal website. A **portal** is a versatile and useful website, offering a search engine, indexes, lists, directories, and links to all kinds of stuff. Often people use a portal site for their Web browser's home page—the website that the browser takes them to automatically when they open the browser software and go online.

2.4 USING ONLINE INFORMATION SERVICES

There are several ways to gain access to the Internet, the World Wide Web, and e-mail services. If you are using a college's computer network, you have a direct connection to Internet services. If, however, you are connecting from home or office, you need some form of commercial service, which usually charges a fee for access to the Internet.

LEARNING THE *lingo*

browser An application designed for viewing websites and displaying graphics files and Web documents.

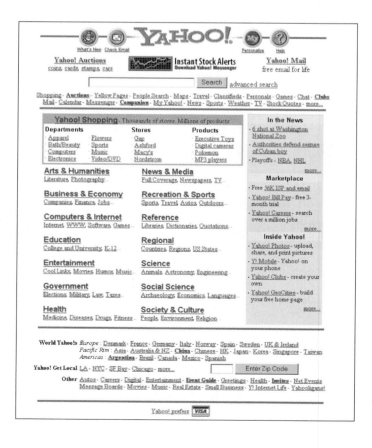

using THE WEBSITE'S MENUS ARRANGED BY VARIOUS CATEGORIES

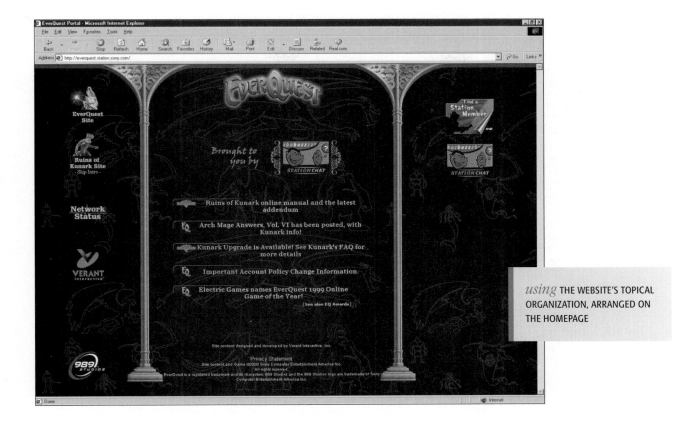

using THE WEBSITE'S TOPICAL ORGANIZATION, ARRANGED ON THE HOMEPAGE

2.5 USING WEB BROWSER SOFTWARE

The Web **browser** is an application that was developed specifically for using the World Wide Web. The first browser was called Mosaic and led to the development of Netscape Navigator, the first commercial browser available. Another popular browser is Microsoft Internet Explorer.

Browsers are simple and fun to use. You don't create anything in a browser, as you do with word processing or a spreadsheet. Browsers are just for viewing, most commonly Web pages, graphic image files, and Web documents. When you start your browser (you must be online), it automatically opens the home page website you have selected. Then you can type in the URL for any other website you wish to visit.

PC & You   ○ *FREE INTERNET ACCESS*
   ○

How would you like to surf the Web and get your e-mail for free? Well, you can. Free Web access is provided by a number of companies. You can get free high-speed Internet access in the United States and Canada. All you need to do is download the application software and install it. One restriction might be having a local free phone number in your area. You must provide a demographic profile of yourself, which is used by advertisers. And the catch is that you must view banner ads, which appear on your screen at all times. Here are some free Internet access services:

▸ AltaVista Free Access, with your own personalized home page (www.altavista.com)

▸ BlueLight, a partnership among Yahoo! and Kmart (www.bluelight.com)

▸ NetZero, which includes free e-mail (www.netzero.com)

THE INTERNET SERVICE PROVIDER, OR ISP, IS USUALLY A LOCAL OR REGIONAL SERVICE OFFERING INTERNET ACCESS TO HOMES AND BUSINESSES WITHIN CERTAIN TELEPHONE EXCHANGES.

TELEPHONE COMPANIES, SUCH AS AT&T WORLDNET, PACIFIC BELL DIALUP, AND BELLATLANTIC.NET, OFFER INTERNET ACCESS. IT IS OFTEN BUNDLED WITH TELEPHONE SERVICE.

three ONLINE INFORMATION SERVICES

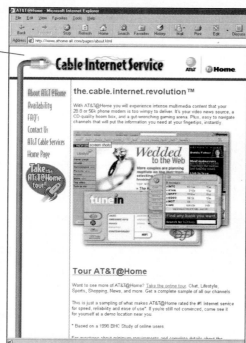

AMERICA ONLINE, OR AOL, IS THE LARGEST COMMERCIAL ACCESS SERVICE. IN ADDITION TO OFFERING INTERNET ACCESS, AOL IS A PORTAL OFFERING ITS OWN ONLINE INFORMATION AND SERVICES.

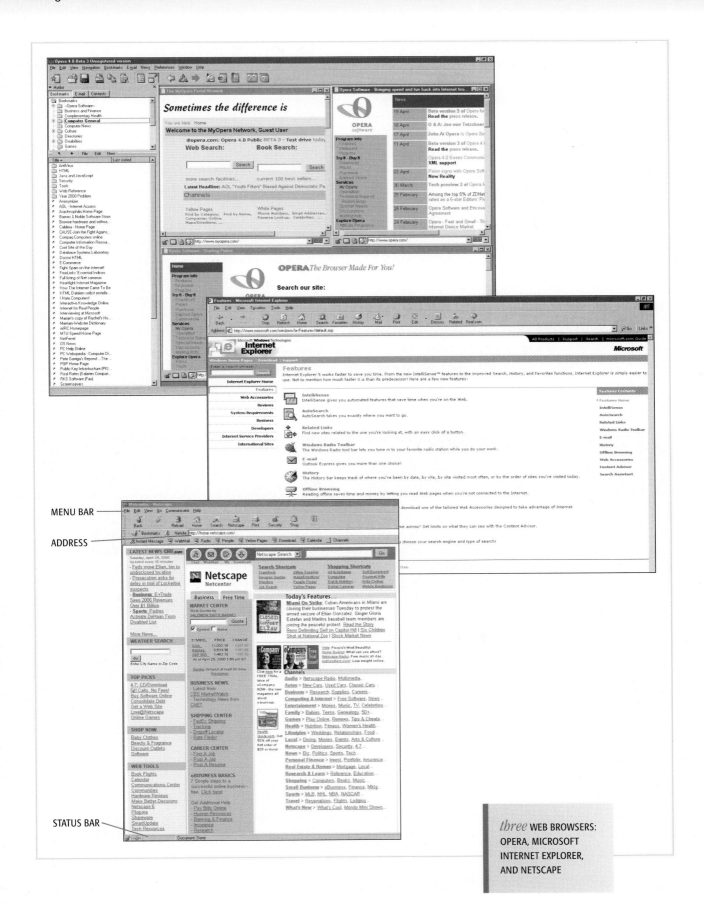

MENU BAR

ADDRESS

STATUS BAR

three WEB BROWSERS:
OPERA, MICROSOFT
INTERNET EXPLORER,
AND NETSCAPE

Working with a Browser. Browsers work very much like all the other software applications, except they're intuitively easier to use. In the center is the *work screen*, where the Web page or file is displayed. You have several tools available for working with the browser. Take a look at the Web browser screens on the previous pages and identify the work screen and tools as you familiarize yourself with the browser.

- The *menu bar* is where you'll find tools for working with files or changing the way your browser works.

- The *Address* or *Location window* is where you type in the URL.

- The *status bar*, just below the work screen, lets you know what the browser is doing, such as downloading a Web page. When you issue a command, you can actually see it identify and display individual files. When the entire page is displayed, the status bar reads "Done."

Browsers are primarily used to view Web pages, but you can also view files stored on your PC or files you receive from others. For example, say a friend sends you a photo over e-mail. If you double-click on the file, your Web browser will open and display the photo. You can also send a Web page as a file attachment with an e-mail.

Browsing Web Documents. Typically, a Web document is a file created expressly for viewing on a website. It has been designed using colors and motifs for the background, different typefaces and type sizes for text, graphic images, animations, sounds, and other multimedia effects. These files are generally characterized as hypertext, as you learned earlier. They are created using a programming language called hypertext markup language, or html. Often you'll see a website page name with the suffix .html or .htm behind it. When you visit a website, you are viewing an html document. You can also view html documents on your own PC and, in some cases, you

PC & You ○ ○ LET YOUR BOT DO YOUR SHOPPING

The latest and greatest rage is online shopping, or e-commerce, which we learned about in Chapter 1. The only problem is how to find what you want and how to get the best deal. Prices vary. Some websites have low prices but charge high shipping and handling fees. What you need is a helper, and that helper is called an intelligent agent, or bot (short for robot).

A bot is a website that does your price comparison shopping for you. Bots are changing the way sellers sell, because everyone has to keep up with the competition. This benefits you, the consumer, especially when you can compare prices from a bunch of merchants all at the same time.

When you go to a shopping bot, you're asked to type in the name of the product you're looking for. The more information you have, such as the model number, the better. To help you shop, products are often grouped into categories. Some bots offer a hyperlink to product reviews as well. Once you've selected the product, a list of the best prices appears on the screen, with hyperlinks to the merchants for purchasing. Some of the leading shopping bots are:

▸▸ www.mysimon.com

▸▸ www.evenbetter.com

▸▸ www.dealtime.com

▸▸ Yahoo! Shopping http://shopping.yahoo.com/

Don't confuse shopping bots with shopping portals. Shopping portals are like a retail store, selling directly to you, as do individual merchants. But don't overlook individual merchant sites, where you might find great deals in reconditioned, close-out, and auctioned merchandise.

can make a copy of an html file from a website and save it on your computer using your Web browser software.

2.6 USING E-MAIL

Electronic mail, or **e-mail,** is the most widely used computer application. E-mail is a *service* provided over the Internet and you need a software application to use it. This application is what we generally refer to as "e-mail," but it's an application just like Web browsers, word processing, and presentation graphics. In fact, several browsers have a built-in e-mail application.

E-Mail Addresses. In order to send an e-mail message, you must know the other party's e-mail address. There are two parts to the address: the person's name or nickname and the name of the computer, or server, on which their account is stored. The two names are separated by the @ sign. Therefore, a typical e-mail address looks like this: nyoung@reprisemusic.com.

You can make your e-mail very efficient if you set up your program according to your personal preferences. Preferences include the address book, mailboxes, checking for mail, signatures, and privacy.

- *Address book*. Create an address book containing the e-mail address of everyone you correspond with. That way you can just click on a name when you want to write someone.
- *Mailboxes*. Your program comes with an inbox, outbox, sent mailbox, and deleted mailbox. You can however,

create your own mailboxes to keep correspondence from certain people or on specific topics.

- *Checking for mail*. If you're online a lot, you might want to set up your e-mail program so that it checks for new messages at specific intervals, for example every 15 minutes.
- *Signature*. Your e-mail program will automatically insert text you create in every message you send. This is usually called a signature, since it is commonly information about you—your name, address, phone number, and so forth—although you can create anything you like.
- *Privacy*. Some e-mail programs have the ability to *encrypt*, or code your message so that no one except the person you're sending it to can read it. However, both you and the recipient must be using the same encryption program.

Types of Messages. There are two types of e-mail messages. One is simply text, typed into the work screen in the application. Once you have addressed the e-mail and typed in a subject, you simply type your message in the message screen.

The second type of message is called an **attachment**, which is a file you send along with a standard message (although you don't necessarily have to write anything in the work screen). Using attachments is a very handy way to send a file, such as a PowerPoint presentation, since it can be preserved in the format in which it was created.

PC *&* You ⁘   *GOING INTERACTIVE*

One of the greatest things about the Web is its interactivity. *Interactive* means you and the media engage with each other to change the way you use the media. Interactivity is something television always promised but never delivered. Computers, like television, were passive at first, relying solely on humans to make things happen. Not any longer.

One of the simplest ways for you to experience interactivity occurs when you make a mistake or issue a certain type of command that elicits a response from the computer. If you make a mistake, you might hear a warning sound. If you issue a command such as saving a file, you might see a dialog box prompting you to create a filename.

There are many more interesting and actually useful forms of Web interactivity, and they're often a lot of fun. Here are some of forms of interactivity on the Web:

▸▸ www.shockwave.com/bin/shockwave/main/frame_set.jsp Macromedia Shockwave games engage you in a 3D reality.

▸▸ www.interactive.com Interactive 3D banner ads invite you to click and play.

▸▸ Duke Nukem Forever, www.3drealms.com and Shopping, www.mysimon.com. Bots interact with people in games and specialized searches, such as shopping for the lowest prices.

▸▸ http://www.currents.net/resources/chat/ Avatars are online characters and personalities you create to visit cyberspace worlds.

Many sites that sell or purvey books, movies, or music invite you to write your own reviews or participate in ratings and surveys.

▸▸ Check out the book review of William Gibson's cyberpunk novel, *Neuromancer:* www.amazon.com.

▸▸ See some interactive software demonstrations at www.shockwave.com/bin/shockwave/main/frame_set.jsp.

▸▸ Register your rating for old-time science-fiction and mystery radio drama at www.scifi.com/set/classics/boy/.

▸▸ Find interactive feedback channels, such as e-mail, polls, and surveys at www.abcnews.go.com (click INTERACTIVE).

▸▸ Check out www.ebay.com (an auction in progress).

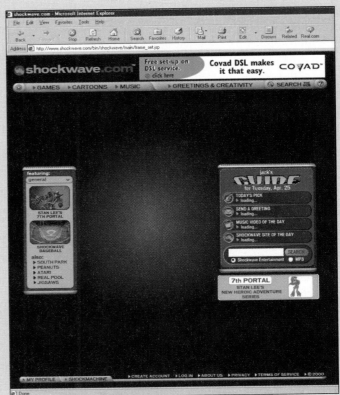

new INTERACTIVE USES FOR THE WEB ARE APPEARING ALL THE TIME.

talking°issues

WHO CAN READ YOUR E-MAIL?

Who can read your e-mail? Just about anyone. According to Tara Lemmey, director of the Electronic Frontier Foundation (www.eff.org), your e-mail messages are about as secure as sending a postcard through the mail. If you work for someone and use your employer's computer system to send e-mail, your employer has the right to read your messages. Personal telephone calls may not be monitored; if they are, or you must be notified that you are being monitored. This is not the case with e-mail. "Until we have better laws in place to protect privacy in the workplace, it is best to assume that your communications can be monitored and act accordingly," says Ms. Lemmey.

Is it possible to protect your e-mail? "You can use encryption to protect the privacy of your e-mail at work, but this is not really a good solution," she says. "Even if you use encryption, the employer can require you to decrypt the message or face the consequences."

Even if you don't work for a company, your e-mail can be read by people whose computers the messages pass through, although it's unlikely that many have the time or interest to do so. But if you really want security, you ought to install an encryption program, such as PGP or Pretty Good Privacy, which is free.

Zero-Knowledge Systems of Montreal has released Freedom 1.0, a for-sale software product designed to allow you to maintain total anonymity on the Net whether on e-mail, in a chat room, or surfing the Web. "It is impossible for anyone—including Zero-Knowledge—to know where you are," says CEO Austin Hill. "You have totally untraceable pseudonyms. You can send and receive e-mail and it's impossible for anyone to know that identity."

If you use America Online and wish to control the "junk" e-mail (often called "spam") you receive you can click on Preferences, then Marketing, then on the right side of the page where there are six categories, including e-mail. Change the preferences for each one as to whether or not you want to receive "special offers" from AOL. Source: ZDTV's "Call for Help"

NETIQUETTE

Everyone is different, from the way we walk to the way we talk. It's often difficult to understand how people feel, or exactly what they're trying to express, when they're speaking. So what about when they write an e-mail message? As it can be very easy to misinterpret or misunderstand, a bunch of people got together (online) and figured out some *netiquette*, or "net etiquette," polite ways to communicate with each other in written e-mail messages. Here are a few things they came up with:

1. Who are you writing to? Before you write, think about your reader, yourself, and your image. Remember, the person on the other side is human. Make sure your communications uses a tone and language they will understand and appreciate; the way you write to your teacher is probably not the same way you write to a fellow student.

2. R-E-S-P-E-C-T. Treat e-mail you receive from others as personal, private, and confidential, unless they specifically give you permission to share it with others.

3. Observe the copyright © and license agreements of materials written by others. If you quote someone from a book or magazine, mention your source.

4. DON'T SHOUT. Typing messages in ALL CAPS = shouting. A single word in uppercase for emphasis is fine, but not much more.

5. *Pls rply.* Use abbreviations sparingly; overuse can make it difficult to understand your message.

6. *You laughing at me?* Be careful with humor. Use *emoticons*, or smileys, such as : -) or the <g> symbol for "grin" if you think your tone is unclear or to reinforce that you're being friendly or kidding around.

7. *Quick!* Reply promptly to e-mail received from others. Let them know their message got through and that you value their correspondence.

8. *Wheat, no chaff.* When replying to specific topics in another person's message, include only the pertinent phrases or sentences. Don't return the entire message in your reply—it is a waste of resources and usually unnecessary. Preface reply portions with a caret >.

9. *Oops!* If you receive a message that was intended for another, either return it to its sender or forward it to the recipient, but let both parties know you received it in error.

10. *Cool it.* Don't *flame*, or reply to a provocative message when you're emotionally distraught. Wait a while to cool down before answering. Always assume that every word you send is part of a permanent document. Don't say something you'll be sorry for later.

11. *Be sociable.* Before participating in chat rooms, forums, or e-mail on services such as America Online or Prodigy, make sure you're familiar with their rules of netiquette.

chapter REVIEW

DO-IT-YOURSELF SUMMARY

1. The world's biggest computer system is the _____.

2. Whenever two or more computers are connected together, they are in a _____.

3. The _____ is one of several services available on the Internet.

4. The Uniform Resource Locator, or URL, is a unique _____ for a computer on the Web.

5. Clicking on a _____ allows you to jump from one Web page or website to another.

6. A _____ _____ is one way to find information when you don't know precisely which website it resides on.

7. A website that provides hyperlinks to many other websites is called a _____.

8. America Online is the largest _____ _____ _____.

9. _____ is the most widely used computer application.

10. Junk e-mail is often referred to as _____.

KEY TERMS REVIEW

a. attachment
b. browser
c. domain name system
d. e-mail
e. hyperlink
f. Internet
g. network
h. portal
i. search engine
j. Uniform Resource Locator (URL)
k. World Wide Web

___ 1. A worldwide computer system and network.

___ 2. Two or more computers connected together.

___ 3. Graphical service presenting information on the Internet.

___ 4. The address of a computer on the Web.

___ 5. The addressing system for websites.

___ 6. A connection between Web pages or websites.

___ 7. Software that finds sites and information.

___ 8. A site with links to many other sites.

___ 9. Application used for viewing websites.

___ 10. Application for sending messages on the Internet.

___ 11. A file clipped to an e-mail message.

KEY CONCEPTS REVIEW

a. bot

b. domain

c. encryption

d. gateway

e. http

f. interactive

g. internet service provider (ISP)

h. netiquette

i. online information service

j. site search

k. subject search

____ **1.** The command used to tell the computer to look for websites.

____ **2.** .edu is one.

____ **3.** A commercial service offering access to online services and the Internet.

____ **4.** Looking for a specific topic or type of information.

____ **5.** Looking for a particular website.

____ **6.** A website or service that offers access to other websites.

____ **7.** A local or regional service offering access to the Internet.

____ **8.** An online tool that finds information for you.

____ **9.** A means of protecting messages from being read.

____ **10.** Engaging with the computer and the media being presented.

____ **11.** Proper manners and behavior when using e-mail.

ANSWERS: 1. e; 2. b; 3. i; 4. k; 5. j; 6. d; 7. g; 8. a; 9. c; 10. f; 11. h.

HANDS-ON EXERCISES

1. Learn more about your browser. Visit all the following websites.

www.bigyellow.com

www.corbis.com

www.broadcast.com

www.cnet.com

www.sports.yahoo.com

www.lowestfare.com

www.startrekcontinuum.com

Once you have visited each of them, click on the small downward-pointing arrow just to the right of the Back button on your browser. Answer these questions:

What do you see?

How would this be helpful to you?

What additional useful information might be available here?

2. Type in the name of one of the sites, but type slowly. Watch what happens in the drop-down box just below your typing.

What do you see?

How would this be helpful to you?

What additional useful information might be available here?

3. With the first site on your screen, click on Favorites and save it. Then save several more websites in different folders, so you know how to do it.

SIX COMMONLY USED OPERATING SYSTEM COMMANDS

SIX COMMONLY USED OPERATING
SYSTEM COMMANDS

learning
OBJECTIVES

- ✔ Why do computers need an operating system?

- ✔ What aspects of the operating system do people need to know?

- ✔ Why is the graphical user interface important?

- ✔ How does the operating system organize our work and information?

- ✔ What is the software that people use most frequently called?

- ✔ What type of software is used with both system software and application software?

- ✔ What are the important issues concerning software ownership?

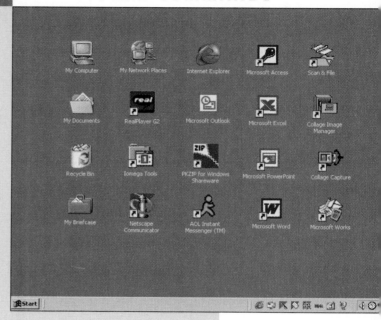

chapter THREE

COMMAND	TASK	HOW TO USE
Copy	Makes a copy of a file	Click and hold the mouse button down and drag the file to the new folder or directory.
Date	Sets the date and time in the Windows system tray	Double-click on the time in the system tray.
Delete	Removes a file permanently from its directory	Highlight the file and either press the Delete key or click on the X.
Format	Creates a usable floppy disk, hard disk, or CD-ROM	Place a disk in the drive and right-click to bring up the menu, then select Format.
Print	Prints a file	Click on the printer icon in the application in use.
Rename	Gives a file a new name	Click on the filename and then click on the File menu; select Rename, then type the new name.

HERE are some of the most commonly used software commands. The applications included in the latest version of Microsoft's office suite work with each other seamlessly through the use of universal commands.

3

USING SOFTWARE

3.1 UNDERSTANDING THE OPERATING SYSTEM

Knowing how to get the most out of your operating system can make a big difference in how you use your PC. There are a number of features and utilities that make your computing more interesting and sometimes even fun.

But these utilities and programs are just some of the side benefits of the **operating system,** or **OS** for short. Let's take a look at the basics—what the operating system does for you and why you ought to be glad it does.

Operating System Basics.   System software and operating system software work together to control and manage

the computer. Refer to the figure as you learn about some of the most important tasks that the OS performs.

3.2 PC OPERATING SYSTEMS

The three most popular operating systems for PCs are Windows, Linux, and MacOS. The operating system must be compatible with the computer's processor. Windows and Linux are operating systems for PCs using an Intel microprocessor, or a microprocessor that works like an Intel, such as the Cyrix or AMD. For that reason, the most popular type of PC is often referred to as a *Wintel—Win*dows and In*tel* combined. Apple Computer's MacOS works only with Macintosh PCs using their own microprocessors made by Motorola and IBM.

Windows.   Microsoft Windows is the most widely used operating system on earth, with over 90 percent of the market. There are currently two version of Windows. The one most of us use is called Windows Millennium, considered the consumer version, and it replaces Windows 98. The other is Windows 2000, the business version, which replaces Windows NT. Microsoft felt it better to

LEARNING THE lingo

operating system   Software essential to basic computer functions, coordinating activities between the hardware and various types of software including applications and utilities.

ACCESSORIES LET YOU USE A CLOCK, CALCULATOR, OR ADDRESS BOOK, OR PLAY GAMES, LISTEN TO MUSIC CDS, AND WATCH DVDS.

THIS OPERATING SYSTEM UTILITY DIALS THE INTERNET OR OTHER ONLINE SERVICES, ENTERS YOUR USERNAME AND PASSWORD, AND LOGS YOU ONTO THE NETWORK.

interesting AND USEFUL OPERATING SYSTEM FEATURES AND UTILITIES

THIS UTILITY SHOWS YOU ALL THE DIRECTORIES, FOLDERS, AND FILES ON YOUR COMPUTER AND LETS YOU VIEW, MOVE, COPY, DELETE THEM, AND LOTS MORE.

FIND WILL LOCATE A FOLDER OR FILE, OR WORDS THAT ARE PART OF THE FOLDER NAME OR FILENAME.

YOU CAN PUT ALL YOUR FAVORITE AND MOST FREQUENTLY USED PROGRAMS IN THE START MENU SIMPLY BY CLICKING AND DRAGGING THE ICON TO IT.

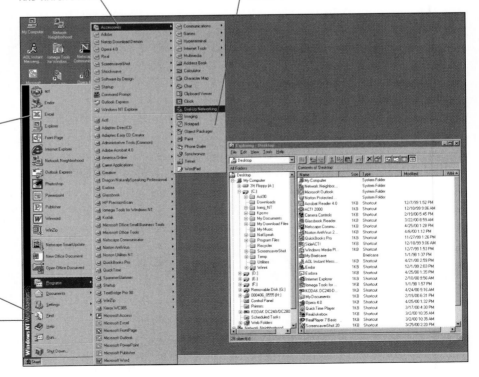

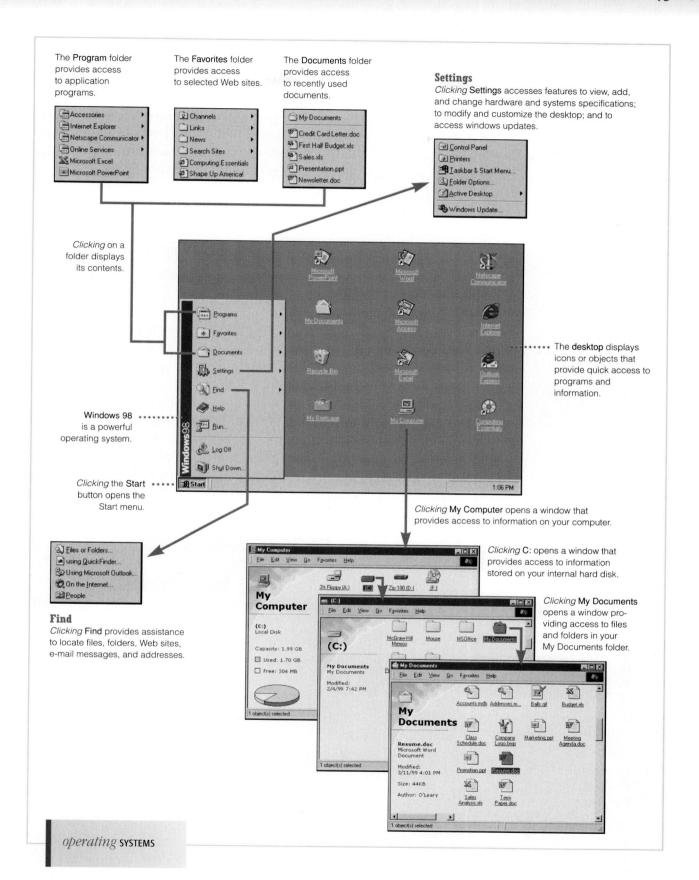

The **Program** folder provides access to application programs.

The **Favorites** folder provides access to selected Web sites.

The **Documents** folder provides access to recently used documents.

Settings

Clicking Settings accesses features to view, add, and change hardware and systems specifications; to modify and customize the desktop; and to access windows updates.

Clicking on a folder displays its contents.

The **desktop** displays icons or objects that provide quick access to programs and information.

Windows 98 is a powerful operating system.

Clicking the Start button opens the Start menu.

Clicking My Computer opens a window that provides access to information on your computer.

Clicking C: opens a window that provides access to information stored on your internal hard disk.

Clicking My Documents opens a window providing access to files and folders in your My Documents folder.

Find

Clicking Find provides assistance to locate files, folders, Web sites, e-mail messages, and addresses.

operating SYSTEMS

have one version for everyone; however, some people may find that Windows 2000 is more sophisticated than they want, so Microsoft has a version called Windows Millennium for them. Here are some of its features:

- Compared to Windows 98, it is nearly crash-proof.
- More multimedia and gaming capabilities.
- Easy to upgrade and install hardware and software.
- Automatically upgrades itself while you're online.

Microsoft Windows has the most applications available of any operating software; for that reason alone it dominates the market. New PCs will likely come with Windows Millennium pre-installed, but if you're using Windows 98, it may not be worth your while to upgrade.

Linux. Most people probably won't use Linux anytime soon, even though you can download a copy for free from the Web. It's an alternative to Windows and a great OS for heavy-duty uses, like running computers on the Internet. It is also very customizable—you can personalize the way it looks and works. But there isn't much in the way of applications available for it yet, and that keeps people from making a switch. Here are some of Linux's features:

- Extremely reliable.
- Able to work with very large (terabytes) files.
- Excellent security, especially for the Internet.
- Very customizable, because it uses the X Windows graphical user interface.

Should you delete Windows and install Linux? It depends on how technologically curious and sophisticated you are. One Linux user says, "If your VCR still blinks 12:00, Linux is not for you."

MacOS. The Macintosh operating system does not compete with Windows or Linux because it's only for the Mac. That doesn't make the MacOS any less an excellent operating system, though, because Apple would love to have people switch from Wintel machines to theirs.

E-Notes
How do people use their PCs at work?

American workers spend 35 percent of their workday using a computer, according to a recent research study conducted by Rutgers University and the University of Connecticut. Those interviewed said they are on the Internet 23 percent of the time; the most commonly used applications are word processing and e-mail—80 percent. When asked about telecommuting (working from home) 41 percent said they would work effectively, although only 9 percent actually do telecommute.

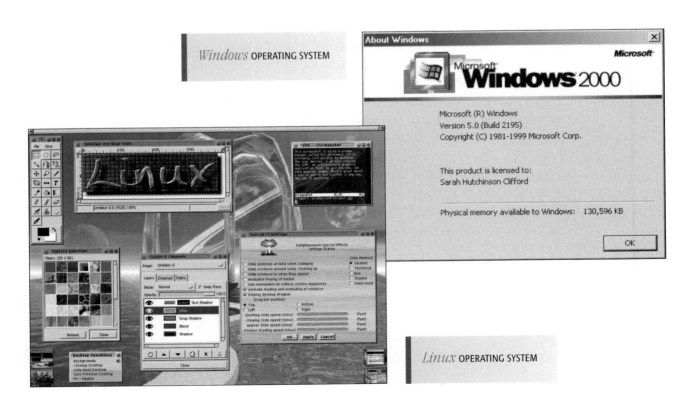

Windows OPERATING SYSTEM

Linux OPERATING SYSTEM

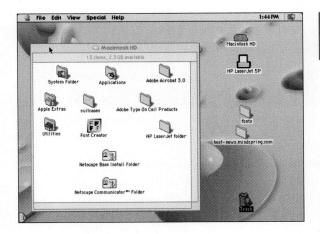

Here are some of Mac OS's features:

- Speech recognition, including a voice password.
- Keychain, one password that remembers your other passwords, such as for websites.
- Sherlock 2, a sophisticated search tool for both files and the Internet.
- Personal file encryption.

MacOS X, the next upgrade, will be a stronger, more stable OS than previous versions. It will also provide even

more support for interactive graphics, video, and multimedia production.

Using the Operating System. The operating system does a lot of things for us, without our issuing commands. The following three things that we actively use or do with the operating system make it easier to work with our applications and information:

- *The graphical user interface (GUI)*, which we use to control the computer.
- *Multitasking*, which we use to control the applications.
- *Managing files and folders*, which we use to work with the information we create.

While often initiated by the application, it is the operating system that manages the data in memory.

The GUI, or Graphical User Interface. One of the operating system's most important tasks is presenting the computer system to you. This is called the **graphical**

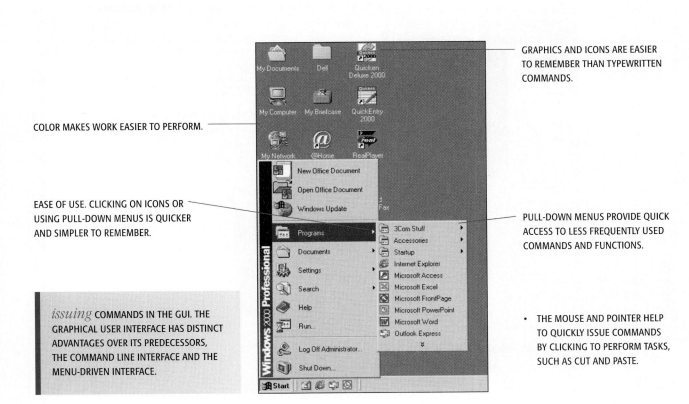

GRAPHICS AND ICONS ARE EASIER TO REMEMBER THAN TYPEWRITTEN COMMANDS.

COLOR MAKES WORK EASIER TO PERFORM.

EASE OF USE. CLICKING ON ICONS OR USING PULL-DOWN MENUS IS QUICKER AND SIMPLER TO REMEMBER.

PULL-DOWN MENUS PROVIDE QUICK ACCESS TO LESS FREQUENTLY USED COMMANDS AND FUNCTIONS.

issuing COMMANDS IN THE GUI. THE GRAPHICAL USER INTERFACE HAS DISTINCT ADVANTAGES OVER ITS PREDECESSORS, THE COMMAND LINE INTERFACE AND THE MENU-DRIVEN INTERFACE.

- THE MOUSE AND POINTER HELP TO QUICKLY ISSUE COMMANDS BY CLICKING TO PERFORM TASKS, SUCH AS CUT AND PASTE.

LEARNING THE lingo

graphical user interface A software design that works on top of the operating system, providing color, graphics, icons, and pulldown menus, and that permits the use of a pointing device to issue commands and instructions.

LEARNING THE lingo

multitasking Opening and using more than one program at a time.

user interface, or **GUI.** The GUI makes it possible to actually use the computer.

When you use the GUI, you issue commands by clicking on an icon with the mouse pointer. Some functions are found in pull-down menus.

The GUI has provided an additional benefit: standardizing the way we work with various applications. A set of intuitive and easily recognized icons and screen features is used in Windows as well as in applications ranging from word processing to graphics to Web browsers. This makes it easier for us to learn many more applications and exchange information between applications.

Multitasking. **Multitasking** lets you use more than one application at the same time. This means you can have a number of different applications and desktop tools open and ready to use at a moment's notice. These applications are displayed on the taskbar (see figure). All you have to do is click on the one you want.

In addition, multitasking allows certain tasks to be performed in the background, without having to wait or monitor them while working at another task in the foreground. For example, if your communications application is programmed to dial out and send or pick up your e-mail every few hours, it will do so without interrupting you at another task. You can also print a lengthy word processing file while working on another.

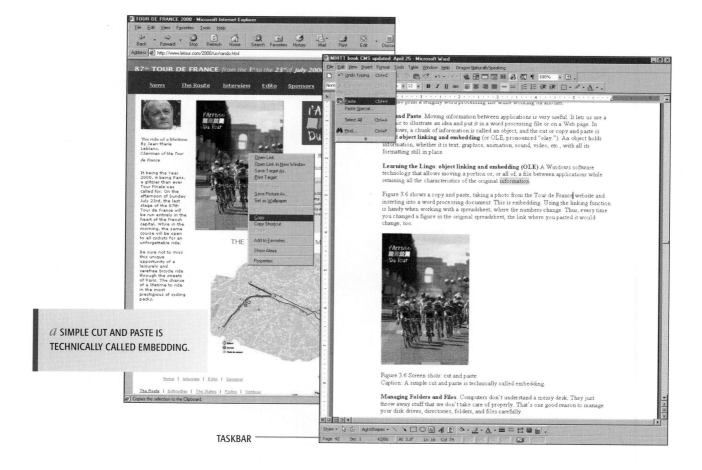

a SIMPLE CUT AND PASTE IS TECHNICALLY CALLED EMBEDDING.

TASKBAR

Cut and Paste. Moving information between applications is very useful. It lets us choose a graphic to illustrate an idea and put it in a word processing file or on a Web page. In Windows, a chunk of information is called an object, and the cut or copy and paste function is called **object linking and embedding** (or **OLE,** pronounced "olay"). An object holds information, whether it is text, graphics, animation, sound, or video, with all its formatting still in place.

The figure on page 46 shows a copy and paste, copying a photo from the Tour de France website and pasting it into a word processing document. This is embedding. Using the linking function is handy when working with a spreadsheet, where the numbers often change. Thus, every time you change a number in the original spreadsheet, the link where you paste it changes too.

> **LEARNING THE** lingo
>
> **object linking and embedding (OLE)**
>
> A Windows software technology that allows moving a portion or, or all of, a file between applications while retaining all the characteristics of the original information.

Managing Folders and Files. Computers don't understand a messy desk. They just throw away stuff that we don't take care of properly. That's one good reason to manage your disk drives, directories, folders, and files carefully.

Windows does most of it for you, installing applications in the proper folder. Windows also helps you organize and store the work you create—information saved in files—in the My Documents folder. It's a good idea to create separate folders for each different kind of information within the My Documents folder. You can create as many as you

> **LEARNING THE** lingo
>
> **file** The primary unit for storing information on a computer. Each application saves and identifies a file with a unique name.

like and give them any name you wish—one for every class, for letters, work, notes, whatever. The same is true for files. Give them a name you'll recognize next time you look in the folder.

When saving your work and creating a new file, remember:

- Shortly after you begin working in an application, save your work by clicking on File, then Save, and giving your work a filename. Save frequently thereafter by clicking on the floppy disk icon.

- You can make the filename up to 256 characters long, so give it a recognizable name.

- Be sure you know where the file is being stored. When you are prompted to type in the name, look to see if it is being saved in the My Documents directory or in the folder you've created and selected.

E-Notes
Saving your work.

The most important thing you can learn about using a computer is how to save your information. All the information we create is stored on the computer in a **file,** which is not managed by the operating system but managed by the application we used to create the work.

managing FOLDERS AND FILES

- THE HARD DISK DRIVE IS WHERE APPLICATIONS AND INFORMATION ARE STORED.

- WINDOWS ORGANIZES APPLICATIONS AND INFORMATION INTO DIRECTORIES.

- AN INDIVIDUAL PROGRAM OR TYPE OF INFORMATION IS STORED IN A UNIQUE FOLDER.

- FOLDERS HOLD INDIVIDUAL FILES.

PC ᴬⁿᵈ You   FOLDER AND FILE MANAGEMENT

People use applications to organize information into files. **For example:**

▸▸ Writing is organized using word processing.

▸▸ Numbers are organized using a spreadsheet.

▸▸ Images are organized by a graphics program.

Even though the file is named and stored in the application, it is actually the operating system that performs the naming and storing task.

You create new *folders* using the operating system, whereas you create new *files* using the application. Here's how to create a new folder within the My Documents folder:

USING WINDOWS EXPLORER

1. Double-click on My Documents, to put yourself in that folder.
2. Click on the File pull-down menu.
3. Click on New.
4. Slide the pointer to the right and select Folder.
5. A new folder, named New Folder, will appear at the bottom of the My Documents directory screen. Type in the name, **Information Technology Today Work Folder** and press Enter.

USING MY COMPUTER

1. Double-click on My Computer.
2. Double-click on the C: drive.
3. Double-click on My Documents to put yourself in that folder.
4. Click on the File pull-down menu.
5. Click on New.
6. Slide the pointer to the right and select Folder.
7. A new folder, named New Folder, will appear at the bottom of the My Documents directory screen. Type in the name, **Information Technology Today Work Folder** and press Enter.

Here's how to create a file in an application:

1. Click on the File pull-down menu.
2. Slide the pointer to Save and click.
3. A dialog box appears. Check the Directory in the Save In box. Use the arrow boxes to change directories if necessary.
4. Begin typing the new filename over the blue text in the File Name box.
5. Click Save or press Enter when finished.
6. The file remains open until you click Close.
7. If you want to save the file in a new version, change the name or add "draft 2" or "second revision" or words to that effect.

Learning good file management habits will save you a lot of grief in the long run. It's important that you save your new work soon after you begin it, giving it a filename. If you don't and you lose power or have a computer problem, in all likelihood you will lose your work.

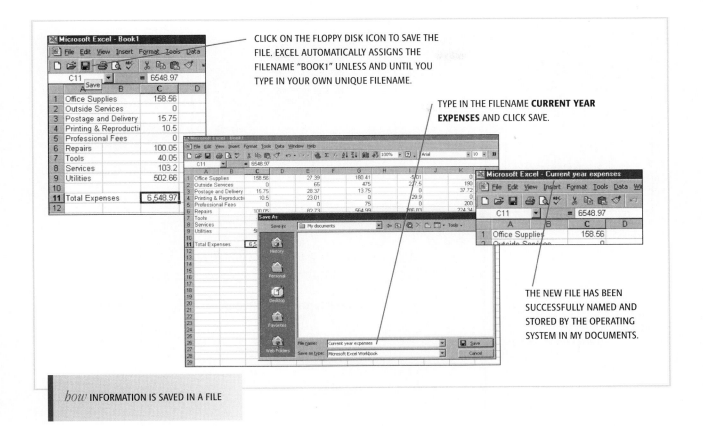

CLICK ON THE FLOPPY DISK ICON TO SAVE THE FILE. EXCEL AUTOMATICALLY ASSIGNS THE FILENAME "BOOK1" UNLESS AND UNTIL YOU TYPE IN YOUR OWN UNIQUE FILENAME.

TYPE IN THE FILENAME **CURRENT YEAR EXPENSES** AND CLICK SAVE.

THE NEW FILE HAS BEEN SUCCESSFULLY NAMED AND STORED BY THE OPERATING SYSTEM IN MY DOCUMENTS.

how INFORMATION IS SAVED IN A FILE

- Save your work frequently, at least every 10 to 15 minutes. You can do this in most applications by clicking on the floppy disk icon or by holding down the Ctrl key and pressing S. Some applications allow you to set up an automatic save interval.

3.3 USING APPLICATIONS

Applications are what we do with the computer. They are the way we get work done and accomplish tasks. Applications are similar to each other because of the graphical user interface design. This similarity makes it easy to learn new applications. But applications differ in what they do for us. Let's take a brief look at the most commonly used applications.

Word Processing. Word **processing** is an application designed to write, revise, format, save, and print documents. Word processing is a tool for working with two primary forms of human communication: ideas and words. Whether writing term papers or letters, composing the lyrics to a tune, or creating a business memo, word processing helps us write more easily. This is because it has

distinct advantages over other noncomputerized writing tools and methods. There are five steps in using word processing: writing, revising, formatting, saving, and printing.

Word processing makes writing, or the process of conveying information with words, easy. Word processing automates many actions we used to perform manually on typewriters. Here are two big differences:

- You can type continuously without pressing the typewriter's carriage return key at the end of each line of text. A word processing feature called *word wrap* does it for us automatically, pushing the text onto the next line.
- You don't have to insert a new piece of paper after each page is finished as you do with a typewriter as a feature called *scrolling* allows you to continuously view the

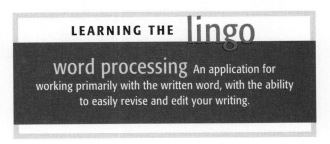

LEARNING THE *lingo*

word processing An application for working primarily with the written word, with the ability to easily revise and edit your writing.

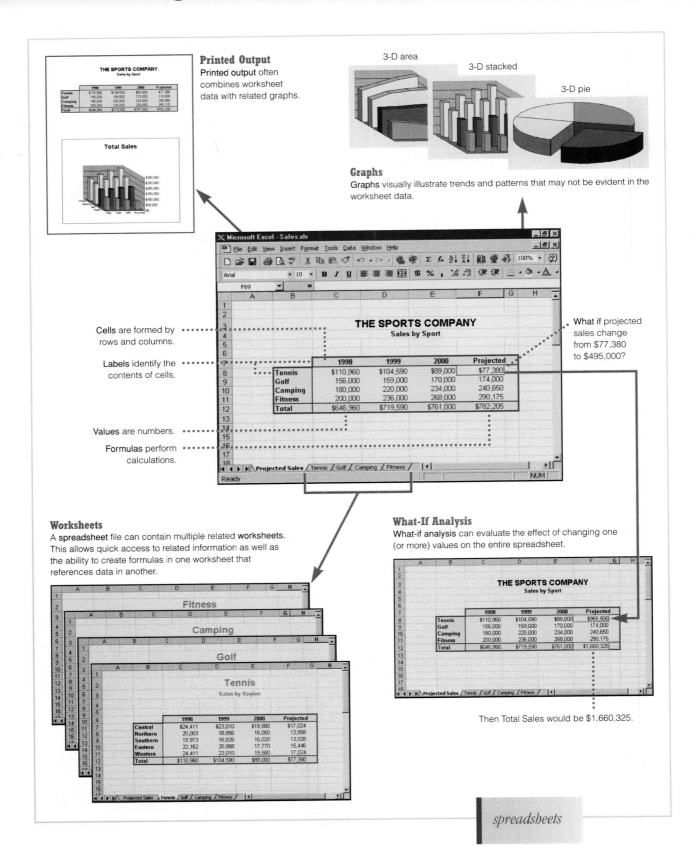

Printed Output

Printed output often combines worksheet data with related graphs.

3-D area

3-D stacked

3-D pie

Graphs

Graphs visually illustrate trends and patterns that may not be evident in the worksheet data.

Cells are formed by rows and columns.

Labels identify the contents of cells.

Values are numbers.

Formulas perform calculations.

THE SPORTS COMPANY
Sales by Sport

	1998	1999	2000	Projected
Tennis	$110,960	$104,590	$89,000	$77,380
Golf	156,000	159,000	170,000	174,000
Camping	180,000	220,000	234,000	240,650
Fitness	200,000	236,000	268,000	290,175
Total	$646,960	$719,590	$761,000	$782,205

What if projected sales change from $77,380 to $495,000?

Worksheets

A **spreadsheet** file can contain multiple related **worksheets**. This allows quick access to related information as well as the ability to create formulas in one worksheet that references data in another.

Tennis

Sales by Region

	1998	1999	2000	Projected
Central	$24,411	$23,010	$19,580	$17,024
Northern	20,003	18,856	16,050	13,958
Southern	19,973	18,826	16,020	13,928
Eastern	22,162	20,888	17,770	15,446
Western	24,411	23,010	19,580	17,024
Total	$110,960	$104,590	$89,000	$77,380

What-If Analysis

What-if analysis can evaluate the effect of changing one (or more) values on the entire spreadsheet.

THE SPORTS COMPANY
Sales by Sport

	1998	1999	2000	Projected
Tennis	$110,960	$104,590	$89,000	$955,500
Golf	156,000	159,000	170,000	174,000
Camping	180,000	220,000	234,000	240,650
Fitness	200,000	236,000	268,000	290,175
Total	$646,960	$719,590	$761,000	$1,660,325

Then Total Sales would be $1,660,325.

spreadsheets

successive portions of a document on the screen. Scrolling is accomplished by using the scroll bars at the bottom and right side of the screen.

Newer versions of word processing allow you to create a document, or file, that contains both text and graphics. You can either save it or print it as a word processing document. This is handy for creating multimedia documents, such as a flyer with a description and photograph of a new product, for example a hiking boot. You can also save your document and post it as a Web page. Common work processing programs include Microsoft Word and Corel's WordPerfect.

Spreadsheets. The **spreadsheet** is an application designed to work with numbers. The spreadsheet application is used to create financial worksheets, which we save as files. Using the spreadsheet involves five tasks: worksheet design, worksheet creation, organizing and revising data and formulas, saving, and printing.

The spreadsheet makes it possible to create a visual, mathematical model of a specific financial situation on the personal computer's screen. A *model* is a mathematical or graphical representation of something that exists in the real world that can be tested or changed without disturbing the original, in the same way an engineer creates

LEARNING THE lingo

spreadsheet An application that simulates an accountant's worksheet for working with numbers and formulas. It combines paper, pencil, eraser, and calculator.

a model of an auto or an airplane. As the spreadsheet model is financial, it involves the use of mathematical numbers and equations.

Say you plan to use the spreadsheet to model your hiking boot company's sales figures. Although people buy hiking boots all year long, there is a peak sales season. The spreadsheet records and stores sales figures by month, demonstrating the peaks and valleys in the sales year. At the end of the year, sales are totaled, costs are subtracted, and the resulting figure equals profits. Now management can use the spreadsheet to plan next year's sales. If the sales force sells 20 percent more than last year, what will the company earn in profits? The spreadsheet will quickly calculate the new figures. It is possible to represent all this information and more in this simple mathematical model using a spreadsheet. The most common spreadsheet, MS Excel, is shown in the figure.

PC and You: WHEN DO YOU NEED TO UPGRADE SOFTWARE?

Software publishers regularly introduce new versions of their programs—operating systems, applications, and utilities. These new versions are usually numbered, for example Version 4.0. Sometimes you'll definitely want an upgrade, such as when you buy a newer computer and the old version of the program or application is incompatible with it. But often you'll be able to get along just fine with what you're already using. The way to determine this is to carefully examine what's changed in the new version. Ask yourself:

✔ *What are the features* that have been added to this version?

✔ *Which features* will I use and which aren't essential?

✔ *Will the new version* make my work easier or my play more fun?

✔ *Are my old files compatible* with the new version?

✔ *How much* does the new version cost? Is it worth it for what I'll get in new features and ease of use?

If you're still undecided, read some reviews of the new software and let them help you decide. Remember, in most cases you don't necessarily have to upgrade.

LEARNING THE lingo

database management system
An application that organizes data into records, in one or more databases or files, so you can organize, access, and store information in a variety of ways.

Database Management. The **database management system** application, sometimes called DBMS, is an application that organizes data in a highly efficient manner. The DBMS is much more efficient than working with paper records and filing cabinets, because we can look at the data in many different ways, turning it into more useful information more quickly (see figure). There are five steps in the DBMS process: database design, database creation, saving, querying the database, and printing.

A database is a group of related records and files. Here's how a DBMS helps you manage data better. Let's say your hiking boot company keeps track of the warranty registrations customers send in after buying boots. One boot model is three years old, and you decide to come out with an improved model. You can organize and sort all the customers who bought the boots three years ago, print out a report, and then send them a letter describing the new boot. You can also post the document on your website.

The DBMS is able to work with both letter characters—usually words—and numbers, and is able to compare and organize them in ways unlike either word processing or spreadsheet software. Common database programs include Microsoft Access and Oracle.

Presentation Software. **Presentation software** is used to create presentations for a live audience and combine graphics and text on screens like a slide show. In addition to working with photos and images, most programs allow you to insert *clip art,* universally recognized images available in books or stored on computer media that you can use in a wide variety of documents.

Some programs prompt you through the process of creating the presentation with a "wizard" helper, or menu screens. This feature allows you to focus on creating and designing content, which is the fun part. Here are the steps to follow in presentation graphics:

1. Determine the type of presentation—business, informal, personal.

2. Create the presentation title page (or slide).

3. Create and lay out consecutive pages as text, or text and graphics.

4. Write, format, and position text.

5. Select and position graphics.

6. Edit and review.

7. Preview presentation.

8. Save.

9. Choose display option, such as Slide Show.

10. Print (optional).

Combining graphs with text for presentation is becoming common practice in today's enterprise. Whether you are introducing the new hiking boot to the sales staff or making a report to your class, representing concepts graphically with a brief written explanation is considered highly effective communication. The most common presentation tool is Microsoft PowerPoint.

LEARNING THE lingo

presentation software An application that combines text and graphics and multimedia animation or sound to present information to others in the form of electronic slides, for example a class report or business meeting.

Presentation graphics software has an additional feature—the ability to format and use the presentation in different ways:

• Summary or outline.

• Speaker's or presenter's notes.

• Overhead transparencies.

• Computer-generated slides.

• Paper handouts.

Desktop Publishing. **Desktop publishing (DTP)** is the process of combining text and graphics into a professionally published format. Desktop publishing lets you compose, design, typeset, and incorporate artwork into a professional-looking document. The process is similar to presentation graphics, but the result is usually printed. Typically, documents include anything from books and

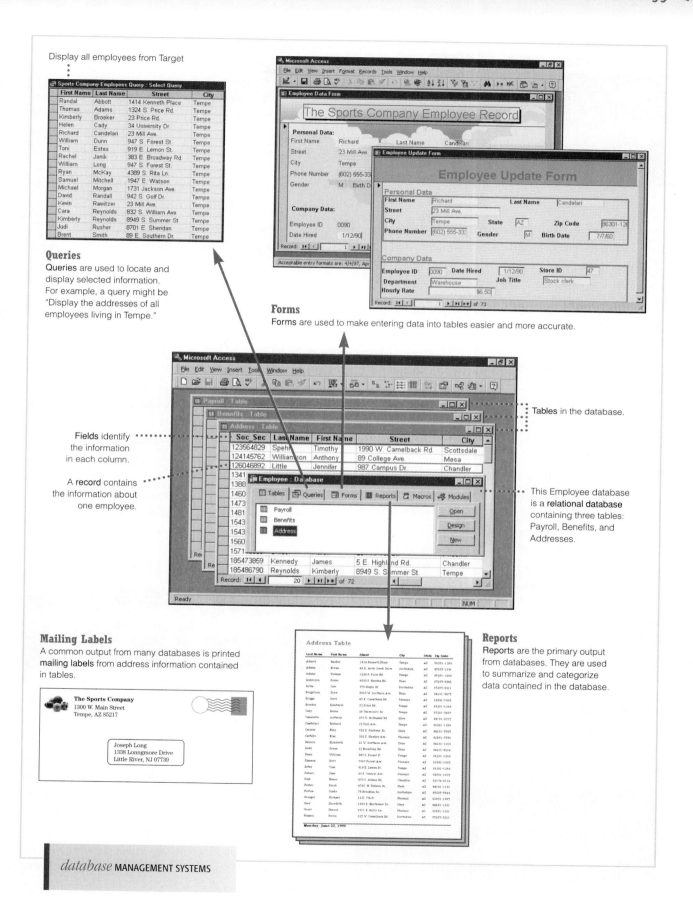

Display all employees from Target

Queries

Queries are used to locate and display selected information. For example, a query might be "Display the addresses of all employees living in Tempe."

Forms

Forms are used to make entering data into tables easier and more accurate.

Fields identify the information in each column.

A record contains the information about one employee.

Tables in the database.

This Employee database is a relational database containing three tables: Payroll, Benefits, and Addresses.

Mailing Labels

A common output from many databases is printed mailing labels from address information contained in tables.

The Sports Company
1300 W. Main Street
Tempe, AZ 85217

Joseph Long
1338 Lonngmore Drive
Little River, NJ 07739

Reports

Reports are the primary output from databases. They are used to summarize and categorize data contained in the database.

database MANAGEMENT SYSTEMS

➡

LEARNING THE lingo

desktop publishing An application that combines word processing and graphics design with sophisticated page format and layout capabilities to create published pages, in either printed paper form or Web page form.

instruction manuals to magazines, brochures, leaflets, flyers, advertisements, newsletters, pamphlets, and even Web pages. The distinction between word processing, presentation graphics, and desktop publishing is blurring.

There are five activities that you, the editor and desktop publisher, perform:

- Designing the page layout, or template.
- Pouring in and copy-fitting text.
- Creating and sizing graphics.
- Formatting.
- Printing.

Desktop publishing creates *typeset* as opposed to typewritten documents. Typically, you write the text in word processing and pour it into the desktop publishing template. Then you add the graphics and charts you created in a graphics program or spreadsheet. You can even include elements from presentation graphics. DTP is often called a page composition program, which means you can design and lay out a document in one or more distinctive page formats. You could design a flyer, a brochure, a catalog, and a Web page using the same text and graphic components and use each in different ways. It's a very versatile application. PageMaker and Quark Xpress are two types of desktop publishing programs.

Web Authoring. Do you want to build your own website? Then you'll need a Web authoring application,

LEARNING THE lingo

Web authoring is an application used to create Web pages and websites, including home pages and additional site pages, combining text, graphics, multimedia video, sound, animation, and hyperlinks.

sometimes called an HTML editor. HTML is the programming language you use to create Web pages, but don't be scared off by that—it's as easy to use as any other application. Designing Web pages is a lot of fun, because you get to select colors, typefaces, and artwork, then put them all together as you design the page. Here are the steps in using a Web authoring application:

- Select the page design or template, if the application makes them available to you.
- Select background designs, patterns, and colors.
- Choose type for headings, body text, and messages.
- Select animations, sound, video, and graphics.
- Choose and create hyperlinks to other pages or websites.
- Save the site pages as files.
- Post the site pages to the website.

Web authoring is the fastest form of publishing. You can post, or publish, to the website as soon as the file is completed. You can also update and revise just as quickly. Say your boot company wants to close out all the remaining stock of the previous model before announcing the replacement. You can have a sale or an auction until the boots are all sold, then immediately take the sale or auction page off the website, replacing it with an announcement for the new boot.

LEARNING THE lingo

paint or draw program An application for creating freehand drawings and illustrations and editing art or photos from outside sources.

Paint and Draw. The most popular graphics applications are called **paint or draw programs,** or just "paint" or "draw" programs. They let you create illustrations and graphics by hand, but also let you edit graphics and usually photographs as well. The images you create can be copied and pasted into other applications, from word processing to websites. The steps in using a paint and draw program include creating a page or design, creating or inserting the graphic art, selecting the display options for the graphic, saving it, and printing.

E-Notes
Free applications on the Web.

The Web browser created a new business model: giving software applications away for free. Sun Microsystems, a leading computer workstation company, is giving away free a suite of applications called Star Office. It is a fully integrated set of applications, including word processing, spreadsheet, database management system, presentation graphics, event planning, e-mail, and an online news reader.

Multimedia Authoring. Creating multimedia includes bringing graphics, sound, animation, text, and video together to create websites, CD-ROMs, and DVD-ROMs. A multimedia authoring application lets you design, create, and animate the visual and sound elements and edit them as well.

One thing a new application must have is compatibility with existing applications, especially leaders like Microsoft Office. For example, Sun Microsystem's Star Office is able to import, edit, print, and export Microsoft Office files as well as files from other office suites from Lotus and Corel.

Star Office runs on Windows as well as on other popular operating systems such as Linux. It is available on CD-ROM or can be downloaded from the Sun website, then installed on your own computer. It can also be run from a website portal, without having to install the software yourself. This makes using it very convenient and it doesn't take up extra space on your hard disk drive.

In the future, it is likely that many more software applications and utilities will be given away from the Web. Even now you can often download a trial version for a period of time—for example 30 days—and try it out. If you like the application or utility, you can buy it over the Web. Microsoft is experimenting with renting applications over the Web too.

3.4 USING UTILITIES

Utility programs fall into two broad categories: those you choose to use for specific tasks and those that perform tasks with other programs, like the operating system. With Windows, an example of the first type of utility is the Web Publishing Wizard, found on the Accessories menu. An example of the second type of utility is a printer driver, which sends certain commands back and forth between the application, the operating system, and the printer, so that your work prints out exactly the way you want. The illustration below and those on the following page show a few examples of the wide range of utilities.

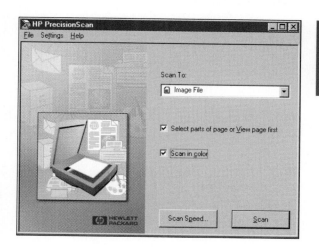

this UTILITY PERFORMS THE ACTUAL SCANNING SO THAT THE IMAGE CAN BE SAVED AS A FILE.

this UTILITY REDUCES, OR
COMPRESSES, FILES TO MAKE
THEM SMALLER FOR SENDING
OVER THE WEB OR E-MAIL.

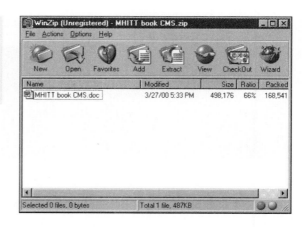

this UTILITY LETS YOU
READ BOOKS YOU HAVE
DOWNLOADED FROM THE
WEB.

talking*issues*

WHO OWNS SOFTWARE?

If you walk into a retail store or call a mail-order company to buy software, you pay for it—but you don't own it. Instead, you've purchased a *license* to use that software, as set forth in the license agreement that comes with it. By virtue of the fact that you've purchased it and broken the shrink wrap, you accept the terms of the license. You ought to read it and see what you've agreed to.

There are, however, several kinds of software not sold in normal commercial channels that reflect what might be called a "people's ethos." The way these kinds of software are sold or distributed places the ethical responsibility for their continued presence in the market and even their improvement squarely on the user's shoulders.

▶▶ Shareware is software that has been developed primarily by small companies or self-employed programmer-entrepreneurs. Like commercial software, it is copyrighted, but it is made available on a trial basis. If you like it, mail your check; if you don't, refrain from using it. Shareware is usually inexpensive.

▶▶ Public domain software is not copyrighted and can be freely distributed without obtaining permission or paying a fee to the author.

▶▶ Freeware is copyrighted software that can be used without paying a fee; it cannot be resold for profit.

Shareware and freeware are often available on the Web at sites like www.download.com, www.zdnet.com (see Downloads), www.tucows.com, or www.shareware.com. You can read brief explanations or reviews, then decide if you want to download your own copy. If there is a fee or an agreement, you'll usually find out up front. The program you download is usually an installation program; that means you use it to actually install the program you want to use. It's a good idea to create a folder just for storing these installation programs so they don't get mixed up with your actual program files. You can even call it "Downloads" if you want. Once you identify that folder for downloads, your Web browser will always default to it when saving files from the Web.

RESPECT AND PRIVACY FOR PERSONAL AND PROPRIETARY INFORMATION

Here are two stories told around the office water cooler. The first concerns George, who leaves his computer on all the time and sometimes finds his screen "looks funny" when he arrives in the morning. It turns out the janitorial staff play some of his games at night. The second concerns Diane, who left a memo with a great new idea that she was drafting on her screen. A ruthless fellow employee copied the file, submitted the idea as her own, and got away with it.

Everybody deserves respect for their rights and privacy, whether on campus or at the office. Unfortunately, it is likely that in the real world unethical people will violate other peoples' rights and read private or personal files. To some extent, security systems should take care of this. As the old saying goes, however, locks only keep honest people honest. What can you do?

▶▶ Don't create temptations.

▶▶ Always keep your work computer secure. Remember, the computer and its data are your employer's property. Log off when you're away from your desk. Conceal your password and follow the company's security precautions.

▶▶ Be sure that all your important work is backed up and stored in more than one physical location (on more than one computer system or on a disk you keep with you).

▶▶ Save your personal files with a password or encryption. As an alternative, keep your files on a separate disk that you lock in your desk or take home with you at night.

Finally, and this is the hardest part, realize that you are part of the problem as well as part of the solution. Encourage your fellow students and employees, through polite conversation and personal example, to participate in ethical behavior. Find mutually shared values and beliefs and don't be afraid to discuss them. People who are basically moral and honest often find it difficult to do wrong to those they know personally. And when you see illegal or unethical things occurring, discuss them with your manager or supervisor. To do otherwise makes you an accomplice to wrongdoing, and it also makes it easier to look the other way the next time it happens.

chapter REVIEW

DO-IT-YOURSELF SUMMARY

1. The software that manages applications and utilities is called the _____ _____.

2. The applications are found by clicking the _____ button.

3. The most popular operating system is called _____.

4. The operating system presents the computer system to us through the _____ _____ _____.

5. The ability to have more than one application open and working at the same time is called _____.

6. _____ and _____ are used to manage and store the information we create.

7. Moving information between applications and files is called _____ and _____.

8. The software we use to accomplish work or tasks is called an _____.

9. Both the operating system and application software use _____ software.

10. Software that you can try and use before you buy is called _____.

KEY TERMS REVIEW

a. database management system
b. desktop publishing (DTP)
c. file
d. graphical user interface (GUI)
e. multimedia authoring
f. multitasking
g. object linking and embedding (OLE)
h. operating system
i. paint or draw program
j. presentation software
k. spreadsheet
l. Web authoring
m. word processing

___ 1. Software that manages the computer system.

___ 2. The software design that presents the computer system for use.

___ 3. Working with more than one application at a time.

___ 4. Moving or copying information between applications or files.

___ 5. The basic unit of information storage on a computer.

___ 6. Text creation and management application.

___ 7. Number creation and management application.

___ 8. Application that organizes data into manageable forms.

___ 9. Application used to present visual and text information to others.

___ 10. Application used to create publications.

___ 11. Application used to create Web pages.

___ 12. Drawing and photo management application.

___ 13. Application used to combine text, graphics, animation, video, and sound.

KEY CONCEPTS REVIEW

a. application
b. cut and paste
c. file
d. folder
e. Linux
f. MacOS
g. privacy
h. saving your work
i. software license
j. system software
k. Windows
l. Wintel

____ 1. Software that manages the computer hardware and operating system.

____ 2. Most popular operating system software.

____ 3. PC designation indicating operating system and microprocessor.

____ 4. Operating system that competes with Windows.

____ 5. Operating system for Macintosh PCs.

____ 6. Process of sharing and combining information between applications.

____ 7. Created by OS, it's where files are organized.

____ 8. Basic unit of storage on a computer.

____ 9. Process of preserving the information created in an application and giving it a name.

____ 10. Type of software used to create and organize information.

____ 11. What you pay for when you purchase commercial software.

____ 12. A basic right that is often intruded upon in the computer age.

HANDS-ON EXERCISES

1. This exercise shows you how to create your own folders. Open My Computer and double-click on the My Documents folder on the C: drive. Now click on File, New, Folder. Create three new folders called Personal, Computers, and Music.

2. This exercise shows you how to use OLE. Start Word and Excel so that you are multitasking. Next, open a sample file in each. Follow these instructions:

To embed information:

1. Use the mouse pointer to highlight a section of the Excel spreadsheet, then click on Copy.

2. On the taskbar at the bottom of the screen, click on Word.

3. Move the mouse pointer to where you want to insert the section from the spreadsheet.

4. Click on Paste.

To link information:

1. Use the mouse pointer to highlight a section of the Excel spreadsheet, then click on Copy.

2. On the taskbar at the bottom of the screen, click on Word.

3. Move the mouse pointer to where you want to insert the section from the spreadsheet.

4.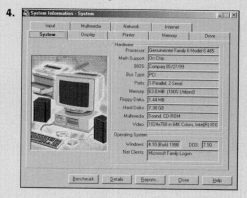

5. Click on the Edit pull-down menu, select Paste Special.

6. Click on Microsoft Excel Worksheet Object.

7. Click on the Paste Link button, then OK.

8. You now see the information from the spreadsheet inserted in the Word file.

9. On the taskbar at the bottom of the screen, click on Excel.

10. Change a number in the worksheet.

11. On the taskbar at the bottom of the screen, click on Word.

12. See that the number(s) have changed.

learning OBJECTIVES

- What is the most critical component inside the system unit?

- What are the two types of memory used for?

- What is necessary in order to connect an input or output device?

- What are the different types of permanent storage?

- What are the different criteria for the amount of storage space?

- What is the most widely used communications hardware device?

- What is the critical issue regarding the use of MP3 files?

chapter **FOUR**

IT used to be that peripherals were a keyboard, a mouse, a monitor, a printer. And while we still need all of them, we can now select from a vast array of peripherals that extend the PC's usefulness, from a microphone to issue voice commands to a surround sound speaker system to listen to CDs while we compute.

TWO innovative peripherals are the Hewlett-Packard CapShare, a portable scanner and copier that lets you store, view, and send information to others. The other is the S3 Rio MP3 player, which captures and stores MP3 files and plays them back. Move over, Walkman!

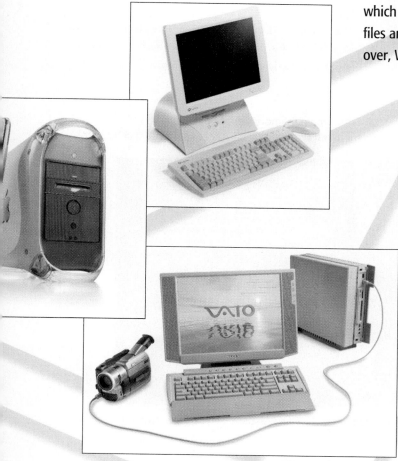

USING HARDWARE

4

4.1 UNDERSTANDING THE SYSTEM UNIT

What happens inside the computer box when you switch on the power? Quite a few amazing things. Everything that has to do with the computer occurs in the box we call the **system unit.** There are delicate and sensitive electronic, electromagnetic, and mechanical devices inside the system unit that must be protected from heat, moisture, and shock. The system unit houses all the critical computer components, helping insure that they will work properly.

Anything that is connected to the system unit or plugged into it externally is called a **peripheral.** The most common peripherals are the input devices, such as keyboard or mouse, and the output devices, such as

LEARNING THE lingo

system unit The box or cabinet that houses the computer's electronic and mechanical devices. It also provides connections to peripherals.

monitor or printer. Other peripherals are the expansion card and storage device. We'll learn about all these in this chapter.

You could say that the system unit *is* the computer. The illustration shows the most common hardware components found inside the PC's system unit.

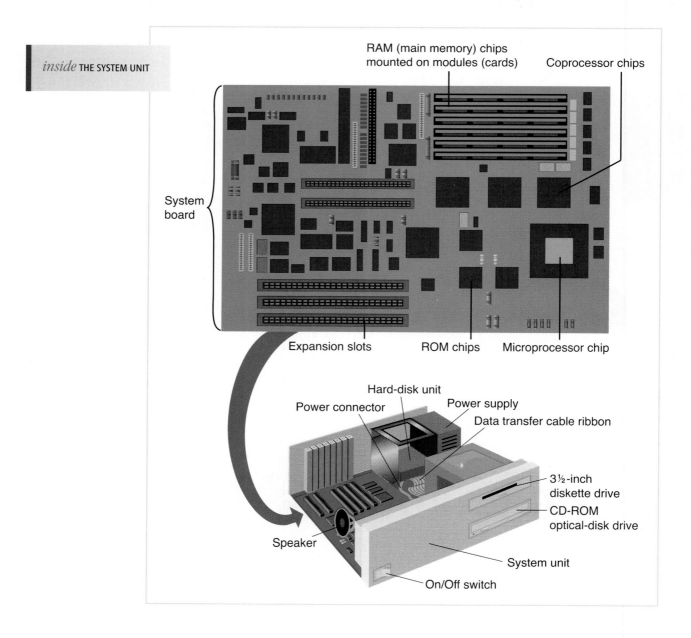

inside THE SYSTEM UNIT

RAM (main memory) chips mounted on modules (cards)

Coprocessor chips

System board

Expansion slots

ROM chips

Microprocessor chip

Hard-disk unit

Power connector

Power supply

Data transfer cable ribbon

3½-inch diskette drive

CD-ROM optical-disk drive

Speaker

System unit

On/Off switch

LEARNING THE lingo

peripheral A hardware component that is connected to the system unit that allows a person to interact with the computer.

- The main circuit board holds many of the critical computer components and connects to all the others.
- The microprocessor is the computer; it does the processing.
- Read only memory (ROM) holds permanent computer instructions.
- Random access memory (RAM) holds programs and data temporarily while you're working.
- A floppy disk drive (secondary storage) is used for small amounts of storage or backup.
- A zip disk drive (secondary storage) is used for larger amounts of storage or backup.
- The hard disk drive (secondary storage) stores all your programs and information.
- A CD-ROM (secondary storage) is commonly used to install programs or for large backup procedures.
- A DVD-ROM (secondary storage) lets you watch videos or movies on your PC.
- Expansion cards, such as the video card, sound card, or modem, plug into expansion slots on the main circuit board to permit other hardware connections.

The Main Circuit Board. Chances are you'll never see it, but the **main circuit board** is where the computer's primary electronic circuitry resides. It's a printed circuit (PC) board that contains a number of *chips* used for processing, memory, routing, and control operations. Think of the main circuit board as a silicon city, where all

the necessary functions and services are found on these chips. The three most important types of chips are explained next.

The Microprocessor. The **microprocessor** chip is the computer itself. It's easy to spot because it's the biggest chip on the board. Sometimes you'll see a cooling fan mounted on it. Another name for the microprocessor is *central processing unit,* or *CPU.*

The fastest microprocessors for Wintel PCs are the Intel Pentium III series, used for the most demanding applications such as architecture, product design, intense scientific or financial number crunching, animation and graphics, and gaming. However, the Intel Celeron chip is completely satisfactory for most of us and is a lot less expensive.

LEARNING THE lingo

microprocessor The PC's computer, or processor, chip.

What if you already have a perfectly good computer, except that it has an older, slower microprocessor? You can often replace the chip with a new, more powerful model, but you must have an experienced technical person advise you on this. The easiest way to find out if your processor can be upgraded is to call or e-mail the computer maker. Tell them what you have and ask what you can upgrade to, or else have an experienced dealer or service technician take a look inside your computer. There are several additional factors that affect speed, so just replacing the microprocessor may not make all that much difference.

LEARNING THE lingo

main circuit board An electronic component where the computer's primary electronic circuitry, in particular for processing and memory, resides. Sometimes referred to as the motherboard.

E-Notes
How much processor speed is enough?

For most applications, such as the Internet and office work, any 300MHz to 450MHz processor is fine. If you plan to work with multimedia or gaming applications, then by all means buy at least a 500MHz PC. The more you work with video, audio, graphics, and multimedia, the more speed you'll want. Since cost goes up with speed, it's often your budget that will do the deciding for you.

processor SPEED CONTINUES TO CLIMB. THE LOW END OF THE SPEED SPECTRUM IS 300MHz, WHILE THE AMD ATHLON AND THE INTEL PENTIUM III IS NOW AVAILABLE IN A 1GHz MODEL.

Read Only Memory (ROM). You know that ROM is called **read only memory** because it holds instructions that can only be read by the computer and that you cannot change. These instructions are permanent instructions, like football rules and regulations, that are used to start the computer exactly the same way every time. ROM instructions are generally stored in integrated circuit chips.

ROM holds the startup instructions, called the "bootstrap routine," that begins when the computer power is turned on. This is what we mean when referring to booting the computer. Each computer's startup program is a little different but, in general, here are its tasks:

- Check the amount of RAM available.
- Make sure the video controller and monitor are working.

LEARNING THE **lingo**

read only memory (ROM)

Memory chips that hold permanent instructions that the computer uses when the power is first switched on. These instructions cannot be changed.

- Assure that external connections, such as the keyboard or printer, are operational.
- Identify auxiliary storage devices and the printer.
- Load the operating system.
- Execute any other instructions it finds on a disk.

ROM is a form of nonvolatile memory, which means it is specifically designed to store data even when the computer is powered down.

Random Access Memory (RAM). RAM, or **random access memory**, is the primary storage area. RAM is directly controlled by the computer's microprocessor. Random access memory temporarily holds the applications you are using and the data or information you're working with while it is being processed. Special chips called SIMMs, for Single Inline Memory Module, are used for RAM.

Random access memory is often called memory, main memory, main storage, temporary storage, or primary storage. All names refer to that fact that it is a working partner with the CPU. Unlike ROM, RAM is read-write memory. That means you can put stuff into it and take stuff out of it.

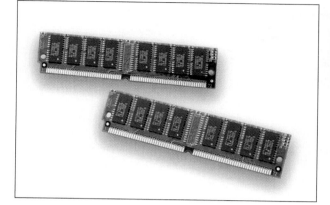

this SPECIAL PRINTED CIRCUIT CARD IS CALLED A SIMM, FOR SINGLE INLINE MEMORY MODULE, AND HOLDS A NUMBER OF RAM MEMORY CHIPS ON EACH SIDE.

LEARNING THE *lingo*

random access memory (RAM)

Chips that hold instructions and data temporarily, while they are in use. The contents of RAM are lost when the power goes off or the system is restarted. Also called main memory or temporary storage.

For example:

- RAM works with the microprocessor to *read*, or obtain, data and instructions, such as when you type characters on the keyboard or click the mouse on a command.

- The microprocessor and RAM also work together to *write*, or transfer, data to other sources such as auxiliary storage. As you shall see, auxiliary storage is read-write memory as well.

Unlike ROM, random access memory is short-term, volatile memory. *Volatile memory* means the instructions and data held in RAM are removed when replaced by new instructions and data. In addition, the contents of volatile memory are lost completely when electrical power to the computer is cut off or if you press the reset button.

Secondary Storage. **Secondary storage** is permanent storage for both programs and data. What you are holding in RAM can be saved on a secondary storage device,

PC *and* You : HOW MEMORY AND STORAGE WORK TOGETHER

Computers differentiate between main storage and secondary storage in terms of speed and efficiency. RAM storage is very fast, because it's usually a chip on the main circuit board, physically close to the CPU. The shorter the distance electrical signals have to travel, the faster the processing. Secondary storage is usually slower, not solely because of the electrical distance but because it involves some type of mechanical operation. For instance, disk drives must spin the disk to store and retrieve data.

Consider this analogy to compare the speed and efficiency of RAM versus secondary storage. A 20-second storage job in RAM takes:

▶▶ 51 days on the average floppy disk drive, or

▶▶ 2½ years on the average CD-ROM drive.

A secondary storage device is a hardware component that has the ability to read and write data and instructions, just as RAM does. One big difference between the two is that secondary storage is long-term, if not permanent.

like a disk. Once data or information is saved in secondary storage, it can be recalled again and again. Applications are stored on secondary storage too, and can be recalled whenever you want to use them again. We'll go into secondary storage in more detail later in this chapter. For now, remember that secondary storage devices are housed in the system unit.

Let's use word processing to write a short memo so we can see how primary storage, or RAM, and secondary storage, such as the hard disk drive, work together.

- *Input.* You type a short memo that reads, "Mountain bike club rides at 3:00 p.m. today."

Comparing the Characteristics of Memory and Storage

	Primary Storage	Secondary Storage
Alternate name	main memory	auxiliary storage
Storage medium	RAM (SIMM chips)	disk
Storage medium is	volatile	nonvolatile
Type of storage	temporary	permanent
Location	main circuit board	peripheral (storage) device

- *Processing.* The CPU executes the instructions to turn the keystrokes into characters.
- *Output.* The characters are displayed on the monitor.
- *Primary storage.* The memo is stored temporarily in RAM.
- *Secondary storage.* At this point, you could also send the memo from RAM's working memory to a secondary storage device, where you could save it permanently on the hard drive.

Expansion Slots and Cards. Those odd-looking plug-in sockets at the left rear of the main circuit board are called *expansion slots*, into which expansion cards are inserted. An **expansion card** is a printed circuit card with circuitry that

LEARNING THE lingo

secondary storage Hardware devices that allow you to save and store your work, which is temporarily being held in RAM, permanently on some form or storage media, such as a disk.

PC and You : UPGRADING YOUR SOUND CARD

Not too many years ago, the only sound a PC made was a "Beep!" from a little speaker built into the system unit case. Today you can listen to all kinds of entertainment from websites. You can listen to your music CDs (or custom music CDs you can make on your PC), and you can download and listen to MP3 tunes. The modern personal computer is, in fact, also a personal stereo.

If you really like to listen to music on your PC, you should get one of the new sound cards, such as the Creative Technology Soundblaster Live. This can reproduce music in digital surround stereo and, with a good speaker system, such as the Cambridge Soundworks satellite and subwoofer system, you will not be disappointed. A sound card makes all the sounds that accompany computer games more dramatic and realistic. If your PC has a DVD-ROM drive, you will be able to watch movies or concerts with all the soundtrack quality of a home theater. You can connect musical instruments or MIDI devices through your sound card, too. And, with the microphone plugged into your sound card, you can have live voice chats with your friends over the Internet.

Your sound card comes with software that is used to install your sound card on your computer. Be sure to turn the power off and follow the installation instructions very carefully, as it is possible to damage the card or slot, or zap electronic circuits with static electricity. Plug in the speakers, put a music CD in the CD-ROM drive, and you're listening to music on your PC. There is often additional software that comes with the card that turns your PC into a recording studio. This allows you to record music from CDs and create custom mixes, including your voice or other sound effects.

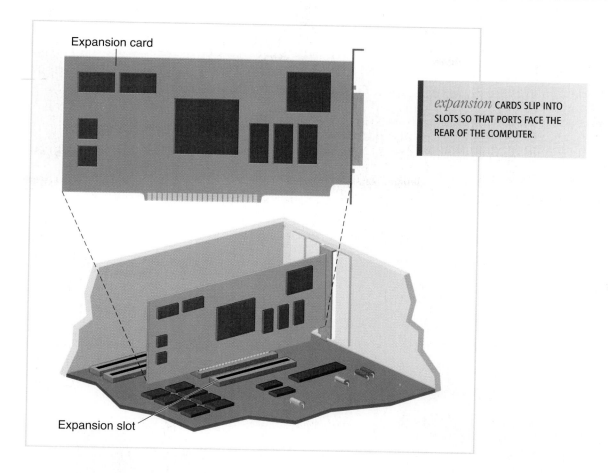

Expansion card

expansion CARDS SLIP INTO SLOTS SO THAT PORTS FACE THE REAR OF THE COMPUTER.

Expansion slot

LEARNING THE *lingo*

expansion card A printed circuit card containing circuits that gives the computer additional capabilities or permits connecting another device to the computer. Expansion cards plug into expansion slots.

gives the computer additional capabilities. You'll often hear an expansion card referred to as an *adapter card*, or simply a card, and the expansion slot simply as a slot. The illustration shows how an expansion card fits into a slot. Some cards are essential, such as the video driver card; it has a port into which the monitor is plugged. The following are commonly used expansion cards:

- Video driver
- Graphics accelerator
- Disk drive controller
- Internal modem

- Scanner controller
- External CD-ROM controller
- Multimedia controller
- Sound card
- TV tuner
- Network interface card

4.2 USING INPUT AND OUTPUT DEVICES

You can't use a computer unless you are connected to it. Once you're connected, you can communicate with the computer: give it instructions, enter data, and get back the results of the processing. This is why we need **input** and

LEARNING THE *lingo*

input device A peripheral used to give the computer instructions or enter data for processing.

output devices—to connect to and communicate with the microprocessor.

How do we connect these input and output devices to the computer? Through ports.

Ports. The **port** is the connection between the computer and external devices, just as an electrical wall outlet accepts the plug for an appliance. Connection is usually made using a wire or cable. To make connecting easy, most ports are designed solely for one type of input or

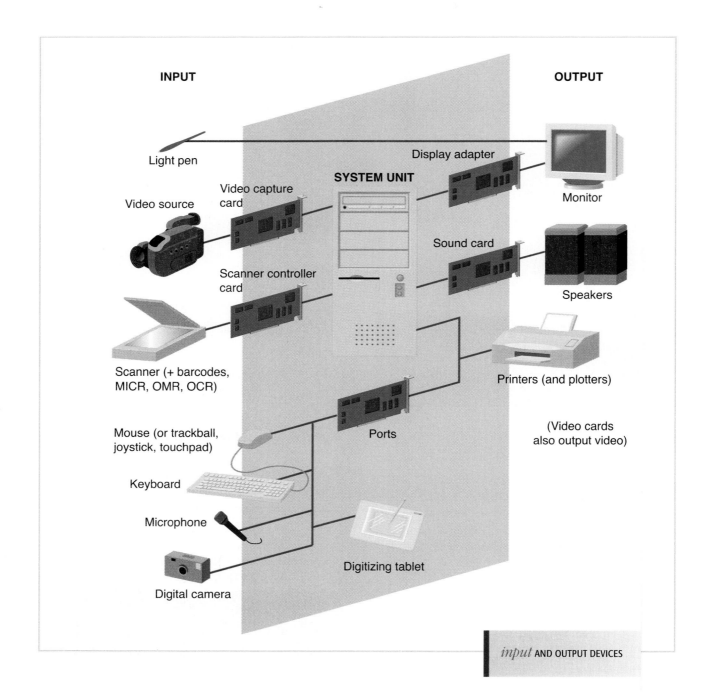

INPUT

OUTPUT

Light pen

Display adapter

Video source

Video capture card

SYSTEM UNIT

Monitor

Sound card

Scanner controller card

Speakers

Scanner (+ barcodes, MICR, OMR, OCR)

Printers (and plotters)

Mouse (or trackball, joystick, touchpad)

Ports

(Video cards also output video)

Keyboard

Microphone

Digitizing tablet

Digital camera

E-Notes

Connecting input and output devices.

While most ports and connectors are unique to one another, it is possible to plug the mouse cord plug into the keyboard port, and vice versa. If you do, you'll probably get an error message on the monitor.

LEARNING THE lingo

hard disk drive A high-capacity storage hardware device that saves data in random order on magnetic disks.

output device. This means it's unlikely that you'll plug the keyboard cord into the printer port.

Ports are arranged along the rear of the main circuit board and provide connections through the back of the system unit. Ports are commonly connections between the main circuit board and the peripherals.

Input and Output Devices. Most input and output devices are controlled and operated by us, people, as we perform our computing tasks. This is in contrast to certain other hardware devices, such as storage or communications, which often perform tasks without our giving them a direct command. Think about how you use each input and output device.

Input devices

Keyboard
Mouse and trackball/pointing device
Joystick (game port)
Microphone (sound card)
Digital Camera (USB)
Scanner (USB)

Output devices

Monitor (expansion card)
Printer (parallel port)
Speakers (sound card)
MP3 Player (USB)

4.3 USING STORAGE DEVICES

Storage devices make it possible to save our work for later use. When we save a file, it is transferred from RAM, or temporary storage, to a more permanent form of media storage. Storage devices fall into two categories: those that use disks and those that use tape. Both are magnetic media. Disks give us direct access while tapes give us sequential access. The CD-ROM drive is also a storage

device, but it uses a laser beam to etch tiny pits into the disk media.

Disk Storage Devices. Disk storage devices use some form of disk, as shown in the illustration on page 70. Disk storage is sometimes called random access as the storage device stores data in a specific location so that any data can be found quickly. This is similar to selecting a song on a compact disc; it doesn't take the CD player any longer to find and begin playing selection 8 than selection 3. Random access is the most widely used secondary storage method. The most common disk storage device is the **hard disk drive.**

Tape Storage Devices. Tape storage devices use magnetic tape on reels or cassettes. Tape storage is sometimes called *sequential access* storage, which means the data is stored and accessed in a particular order as opposed to randomly on a disk drive. This is commonly the order in which it was stored, or else alphabetically or by date and time. Just as you must search sequentially for a particular song on a cassette, so the computer must sequentially search for data stored on tape. Today **tape storage**

E-Notes

How much storage space is enough?

Your hard disk drive capacity should be about three or four times the amount of storage space required by your operating system and application software. For example, if your operating system and applications take up 2MBs, then you should have 6–8MB left to store information you create or work with. This includes downloads from the Internet and working with a lot of images, graphics, and video, which takes up storage space quickly. Some PCs come with a 4.3MB hard disk drive, but for a only few dollars more you can upgrade to 8.3GB and as much as 13GB.

In addition, you should have several types of storage devices, because each lends itself to different uses. For example, if you're going to mail a disk with a few files or copy them to a laptop, a floppy disk is most convenient. Audio, video, and multimedia files are large, so a recordable CD is ideal. Backups are inexpensive and quick with zip disks, LS-120 SuperDisks, or a DAT tape cartridge.

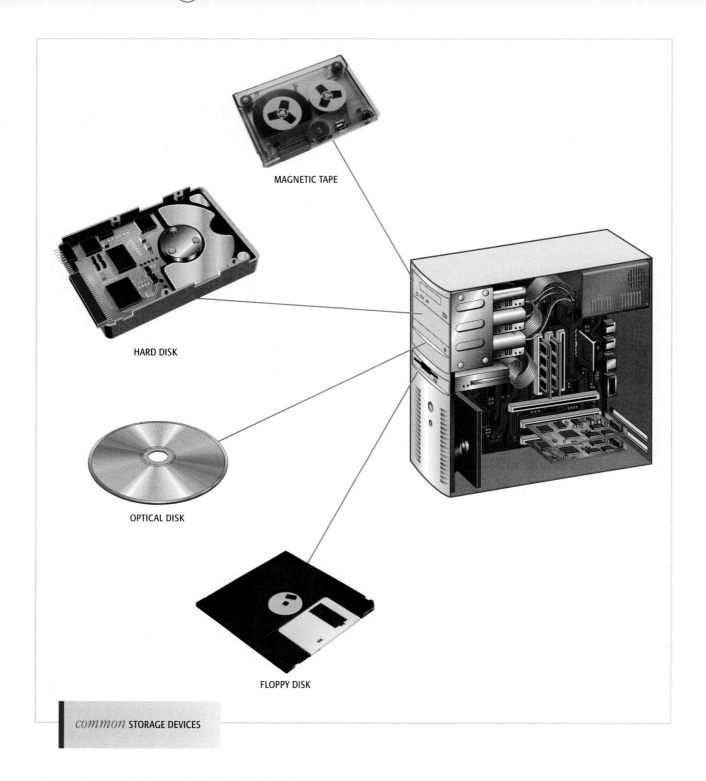

MAGNETIC TAPE

HARD DISK

OPTICAL DISK

FLOPPY DISK

common STORAGE DEVICES

LEARNING THE lingo

tape storage device A storage hardware
device that saves data sequentially on magnetic tape.

devices are mostly used to make protective, or backup, copies of data stored on direct access devices.

CD-ROM and DVD-ROM Storage Devices. CD-ROMs and DVD-ROMs are random access storage devices. They store data on an optical disk in a continuous spiral

types OF MEDIA

LEARNING THE lingo

media The physical material used to store programs and data permanently or for later use. Media may be magnetic or optical.

of bumps etched on the disk, starting from the center of the disk. The laser beam in the storage device reads the bumps on the disk. A distinction is made between a music CD and a computer CD; the latter is called a CD-ROM, for *Compact Disk–Read Only Memory*. The new generation of CD storage devices are also capable of saving your work on CDs. They are termed CD-R, for *CD–Recordable*.

Media. Media refers to the physical material that secondary storage devices use to store data and instructions. Here are the most common types of media used with computers:

- Magnetically coated disks, such as the floppy disk
- Magnetic tape
- Optical disks such as CD-ROMs or DVD-ROMs

The main difference between a CD-ROM and a DVD-ROM disk is storage capacity: a DVD-ROM disk holds almost eight times as much data as a CD. Shown here are the most frequently used types of media. Some types of media and their storage capacity are:

- Floppy disk capacity is 1.44MB and is not often used these days.
- The LS-120 SuperDisk is the same size as the floppy disk, but holds 120MB.
- Zip disk typically holds 100MB and is good for transferring large files between computers.
- Hard disk drives have multiple disks inside that store typically between 4–5GB and 20–30GB, but range up to 72GB.
- Tape backup systems commonly use digital audio tape (DAT) cartridges that hold 30–60GB; they must have more capacity than the hard disk drive they are backing up.
- CD-ROM capacity is 650MB or 74 minutes on a music CD.
- DVD-ROM capacity is 4.7GB—on each side of the disk!

4.4 USING COMMUNICATIONS DEVICES

A communications device lets your PC exchange information with another computer. The one you'll use most frequently is the modem. Another is the network interface card, a communications device we'll discuss in the next chapter.

LEARNING THE lingo

modem A hardware device that connects the computer to the telephone line for communication with other computers.

The Modem. A **modem** is a hardware device that allows computers to communicate via telephone lines. The word modem is a combination of the terms *mo*dulator and *dem*odulator. You connect a terminal or personal computer to a modem and the modem to the telephone line, as shown in the illustration. At the sending end, the modem *modulates*, or converts, the computer's digital signals so they can be transmitted over the analog phone line. At the receiving end, the modem *demodulates*, or reconverts, the analog telephone signals back into digital signals the computer understands.

Most modems these days are capable of sending not only computer data but faxes and voice e-mail messages as well. When the all-digital networks are complete, we won't need to use modems any longer.

E-Notes

Everything you ever wanted to know about modems.

The most common phone line modems are internal and external. Others include:

- *Fast:* The DSL modem is designed for the newer high-speed Digital Subscriber Line phone service.

- *Faster:* The cable modem uses your television cable service.

- *Half as fast:* The satellite modem uses your home television satellite system. Fast on the upload, slow on the download.

- *Slick:* The cellular modem is handy for laptop computers.

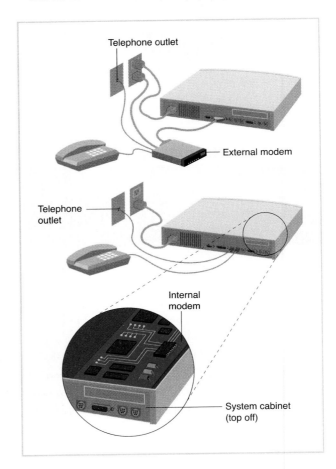

talking*issues*

BUY NOW OR BUY LATER?

A popular online chat group recently received this message from Kelly:

> I need to buy a new PC. It would obviously be more convenient to get my new system sooner rather than later. However, since there will be new microprocessor announcements next month, I am wondering if I would be making a big mistake if I bought now and did not wait.
>
> I worry that if I buy now, prices will drop after the announcements or that the new models may make the current ones obsolete. I could run into some trouble later, especially if I want to upgrade.

Among the responses:

▸ You buy the best computer for the best price, but two weeks later you see a better computer for a cheaper price and you feel like a jerk.

▸ In my opinion, buy now. Prices always drop, and new systems will always make current ones obsolete. That's the way it works.

▸ If you want a new computer now, buy one now.

▸ There's always something new that is better than your current system. If I needed a new system, I'd buy it now.

Many people look at the PC market and see that prices are falling, so they decide to wait to buy a new desktop, laptop, or peripheral. The truth is that since the dawn of the PC, prices have always been falling and they will probably do so for the foreseeable future. Often it's more important to get the advantages of the new PC or hardware device than to save a few dollars. Besides, you'll save a comparable amount on your next purchase.

When it comes to buying computer technology, the best deals are found on the Web and in catalog shopping. You will find the best prices, the widest selection, and often free overnight shipping. One big advantage to online shopping is the opportunity to buy reconditioned, or refurbished, computers and peripherals. These are units that were returned with a problem that was fixed; however, the item cannot then be sold as new. In almost all cases, it's a good deal. Computer components usually break down within the first 90 days, but after that will last practically forever. That refurbished computer has been tested and retested more than a new one; it's going to be rock-solid.

MP3, MUSIC CDS, AND COPYRIGHT

The World Wide Web started an incredible trend in the information business: giving stuff away for free. First it was browser software; hardly anyone had to pay for it and today it's totally free. Then came information itself, information from a book or research company that you used to have to pay for—yours for the asking.

Then an interesting thing happened. People who enjoyed something, for example the novels of a popular author or the photos of a prominent photographer, began posting those works on their own personal websites. Suddenly the United States copyright laws were being broken. This trend has continued with music, which can be copied to a computer and posted to websites as easily as text or pictures.

In March 2000, a copyright infringement lawsuit was brought against www.my.mp3.com by former Beatle Paul McCartney's music publishing company and the Recording Industry Association of America. If you use a Web utility called Napster to find an MP3 song to download, it's probably a song that has been pirated and is in violation of copyright law. That song was probably copied by someone from a copyrighted CD. The same thing can happen with DVD movies.

Today the battle is being waged over what is copyrighted and what is free for public use. Clearly, laws are being broken, and individuals who have broken those laws are being prosecuted and punished. But at the same time, the Internet and the World Wide Web are forcing courts and lawyers to take a closer look at what copyright really means. The laws may have to change with the times.

In the meantime, it makes sense to look at who really gets hurt by violating copyright. Ultimately, it's you and me, because if the business and the artist are losing money due to pirating, they're simply going to raise prices. They may also engage in elaborate encryption, as the videotape movies once did, making it impossible to make legal copies for our own personal use. What wants that?

Saying that "everybody's doing it" is not an adequate response to the problem. Each individual makes his or her own choices, and the choice you make may rub off on the next person. Ultimately, prices will fall or laws will change or restrictions will ease when everyone—the artist, the business, and the consumer—gets a fair deal.

chapter REVIEW

DO-IT-YOURSELF SUMMARY

1. The actual computing takes place inside the _____ _____.

2. The _____ chip is found on the _____ _____ _____.

3. Memory that holds instructions that cannot change is called _____ _____ _____.

4. Memory that holds instructions that can change is called _____ _____ _____.

5. Programs and data are kept permanently in _____ _____.

6. _____ _____ connect peripherals to the main circuit board.

7. An _____ _____ lets you issue commands and enter data into the computer.

8. An _____ _____ allows you to see or use the information that results from the computer's processing.

9. The three kinds of storage devices are _____, _____, and _____.

10. The communication device most of us use is called a _____.

11. Most music available on the Web is protected by _____.

KEY TERMS REVIEW

a. expansion card
b. hard disk drive
c. input device
d. main circuit board
e. media
f. microprocessor
g. modem
h. output device
i. port
j. random access memory (RAM)
k. read only memory (ROM)
l. secondary storage
m. tape storage device

___ 1. Where all the computer electronics are kept.

___ 2. The computer chip that does the processing.

___ 3. Memory that holds instructions that cannot be changed.

___ 4. Memory that holds programs and data and can be changed.

___ 5. Where programs and data are held permanently or for reuse.

___ 6. An electronic device that connects to the main circuit board.

___ 7. A device used for entering commands or data.

___ 8. A device for viewing the results of computing.

___ 9. A physical connection to the main circuit board.

___ 10. A magnetic storage device commonly used for permanent storage.

___ 11. A magnetic storage device commonly used for backup storage.

___ 12. What a storage device uses.

___ 13. A commonly used communication device.

KEY CONCEPTS REVIEW

a. copyright

b. modulate-demodulate

c. nonvolatile memory

d. peripheral

e. permanent storage

f. processor speed

g. random access

h. sequential access

i. storage capacity

j. system unit

k. volatile memory

____ **1.** The housing for the computer.

____ **2.** A device that connects the computer and the human.

____ **3.** Measured in MHz.

____ **4.** Memory that is temporary, only as long as the computer is on.

____ **5.** Memory that retains its contents after power is shut off.

____ **6.** Where programs and data are stored from memory.

____ **7.** Hard disk drive characteristic.

____ **8.** Tape drive characteristic.

____ **9.** Measured in MB or GB.

____ **10.** Processing a signal for a modem.

____ **11.** A law protecting intellectual or artistic property.

HANDS-ON EXERCISES

1. This exercise helps you learn how to locate and assemble all the components and peripherals in a computer system. Go to the MHITT CD-ROM and start the XX simulation. Use the mouse pointer to move and assemble the components.

2. The purpose of this exercise is to learn about upgrading your computer with expansion cards. Go over the list of expansion cards and check off the ones you think you would like:

- Video driver
- Graphics accelerator
- Disk drive controller
- Internal modem
- Scanner controller
- External CD-ROM controller
- Multimedia controller
- Sound card
- TV tuner
- Network interface card

Next, visit ZD Net, the Web computer resource, at www.zdnet.com to read reviews of various expansion cards. Find the best value, or the Editor's Choice, for each and save the reviews in files. Turn in a list of the cards you have chosen and their prices.

ANSWERS: 1. j; 2. d; 3. f; 4. k; 5. c; 6. e; 7. g; 8. h; 9. i; 10. b; 11. a.

VIEWPOINTS:
WHAT IS A NETWORK?

VIEWPOINTS:
WHAT IS A NETWORK?

VIEWPOINTS:
WHAT IS A NETWORK?

learning
OBJECTIVES

- ✔ What makes computer networks useful?
- ✔ What is the most common communications channel?
- ✔ What does bandwidth have to do with networks and information?
- ✔ What is the most important software for using a network?
- ✔ What are the different types of network topologies?
- ✔ What is e-commerce?
- ✔ How can you keep your networked computer secure?

chapter FIVE

"**FOR** you, e-mail and the Internet are second nature; starting your own business will probably mean a website before it means an office lease."

– *vice* PRESIDENT AL GORE, SPEAKING AT THE NEW YORK UNIVERSITY COMMENCEMENT, MAY 14, 1998.

"**COMMUNICATION** is the foundation of society, of our culture, of our humanity, of our own individual identify, and of all economic systems. This is why networks are such a big deal."

– *kevin* KELLY, *NEW RULES FOR THE NEW ECONOMY* (NEW YORK: PENGUIN BOOKS, 1999, P. 5)

"**COMPUTERS** did it. Computers melted other machines, fusing them together. Television-telephone-telex. Tape recorder-VCR-laser disk. Broadcast tower linked to microwave dish linked to satellite. Phone line, cable TV, fiber-optic cords hissing out words and pictures in torrents of pure light. All netted together in a web over the world, a global nervous system, an octopus of data."

– *bruce* STERLING, *ISLANDS IN THE NET* (NEW YORK: ACE BOOKS, 1989), P. 17.

"**IN** the era of globalization we reach for the Internet—a symbol that we are all connected but nobody is in charge."

– *thomas* L. FRIEDMAN, *THE LEXUS AND THE OLIVE TREE* (NEW YORK: FARRAR, STRAUS & GIROUX, 1999, P. 11)

"**THERE** are three kinds of death in this world. There's heart death, there's brain death, and there's being off the network."

– *anonymous* WEB SURFER

5

UNDERSTANDING THE NETWORKED WORLD

5.1 UNDERSTANDING COMMUNICATIONS TECHNOLOGY

You learned a little about networking in Chapter 2 when we discussed the Internet. You know that you can connect your PC to the telephone lines using a modem, which allows the computer's **digital** signals to be converted to **analog** for transmission, then back to digital when they arrive at the other computer. Once two computers are connected, we say they are *networking*—in the same way people network. Computers can share and exchange a lot of services and information, such as the following:

- Viewing websites.
- Watching streaming video or listening to streaming audio.
- Downloading files containing useful information, graphics, music, video, and sound.
- Exchanging e-mail.
- Participating in chat groups.
- Sending or receiving faxes.
- Voice conversations.

LEARNING THE lingo

analog An analog signal is continuous and changes in tone, pitch, and volume, like our voices.

digital A digital signal is a single discrete signal, a steady stream of pulses that do not change in tone, pitch, or volume.

There are many technological things that must occur for all this to happen but, fortunately, we don't have to understand most of it. However, the following aspects are important enough for us to discuss.

Analog versus Digital. Computers are digital and were designed to process digital signals. Telephone systems, however, were designed to carry analog signals.

A series of digital signals makes up a data transmission, like a series of letters makes up a word. When a modem (or FAX) connection is made, you'll hear a high-pitched squeal. This is a carrier or carrier signal, a tone indicating

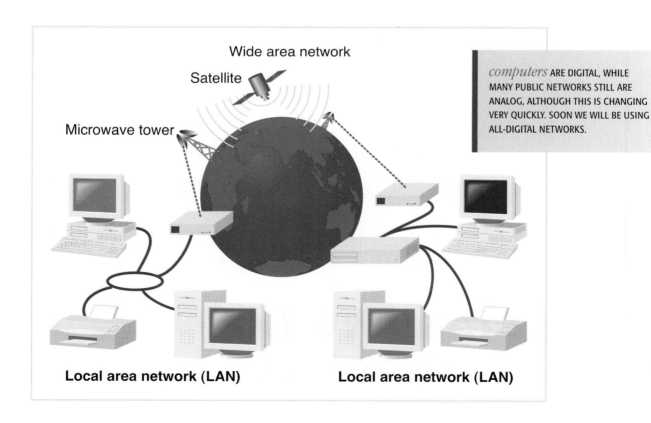

Wide area network

Satellite

Microwave tower

computers ARE DIGITAL, WHILE MANY PUBLIC NETWORKS STILL ARE ANALOG, ALTHOUGH THIS IS CHANGING VERY QUICKLY. SOON WE WILL BE USING ALL-DIGITAL NETWORKS.

Local area network (LAN)   **Local area network (LAN)**

the computer is available. After connection, the carrier signal is modulated to convey the binary information of the computer over the telephone line.

Digital signals are the only language computers understand. The same is true of FAX machines. The illustration shows the differences between digital and analog signals. Most of the communications channels in the United States and Canada today are analog, although this is changing rapidly.

5.2 WHAT IS A COMPUTER NETWORK?

A **computer network** is the way we connect two or more computers together so we can gain access to different information or services. Here's an example of how networks are used on a typical college campus. Your dorm has a small network, as do all the other dorms. There are also small networks for various other buildings or groups, such as administration, the library, the computer labs, and

PC and You: GETTING CONNECTED TO THAT NETWORK CALLED THE INTERNET

If you're connected to the campus network, most likely you're "online" all the time. But if you have to dial a phone number using your modem, you have to connect to use the network and disconnect when you're finished. There are six specific commands and steps that you must take in order to establish an online session on the Internet:

1. *Connect.* When two computers connect using modems, they must be able to understand—communicate with—one another. Modems use their own language to do this. The process begins with the dialer software sending a command to the modem to take the "phone" off-hook, characterized by the ATDT command. AT means "attention," which starts all commands, and DT means "dial tone." You can view this process by using the HyperTerminal utility in Windows to dialup.

2. *Dialup.* This begins the dialup string. During dialup, the phone number is dialed, then you may hear the sound of the phone going off-hook and then dialing. Connection between the two computers is established.

3. *Handshake and logon.* The two computers negotiate the parameters that have been established for a successful connection to begin the work session. This requires an agreed-upon communications protocol. In the case of most Wintel PCs, the communications protocol is called TCP/IP. Because communications require security, we need to enter our user name and password.

4. *Start an application.* A utility software program such as HyperTerminal or the dialer software is used to get connected. However, nothing more will happen unless and until you begin using an application. For most of our Internet connections, the two most common applications are e-mail such as Eudora or Outlook Express, and a Web browser such as Microsoft Internet Explorer or Netscape Communicator.

5. *File transfer.* This means working online, uploading and downloading programs and data, whether it's opening a Web page (typing in an URL to download the file that is the home page) or accessing specific files or data at Internet or Web sites. Some files we download only for viewing (Web page, video) or listening (RealAudio), others to keep (graphics, text).

6. *Disconnect and logoff.* It is critically important to end an online work session by completing the logoff and disconnecting from the phone line. If you do not complete this step, your account is still open and others could conceivably access the system using your logon name and password. It is also possible you could still be accruing access charges if disconnect is not completed.

so forth. These networks are connected to the campus information technology (IT) department computers, which are themselves networked. The IT department's computers are assigned different tasks, such as e-mail, the Web, and various campus computer resources. The e-mail and Web computers are connected to a network—probably from the telephone company—that in turn connects to the Internet. And the Internet, as you already know, is one humungous network itself.

One of the great things about using computer networks is that we rarely know when we are. It's not a technology we have to learn much about, just as we don't really need to know how a telephone network works. That's why networking is often called a *communications infrastructure:* It's a computer system that interconnects us through various communications technologies—hardware, software, and the wiring connections or communications channels.

Arthur C. Clarke, the noted author of *2001: A Space Odyssey* and the man who envisioned the space satellite,

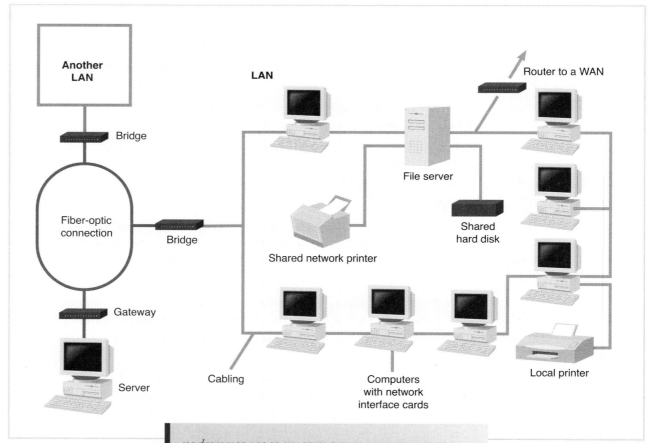

nodes MAY BE A PC OR ANY OTHER TYPE OF COMPUTER, AND EVEN ANOTHER COMMUNICATIONS DEVICE SUCH AS A PRINTER, FAX MACHINE, DISK DRIVE, OR SWITCH THAT ROUTES SIGNALS FROM POINT TO POINT.

once said "Any significantly advanced technology is indistinguishable from magic." That could certainly be said of networking. It's really quite astounding how so many different computers and hardware devices and wires all work together. Some computer networks are private, such as a bank's ATM network. Others are public, such as the Internet. All have these things in common:

- Communications channel
- Hardware
- Software
- Network topology

What Is a Communications Channel?

Quite simply, it's the wires that connect the networks. The simplest network is two tin cans connected with a piece of string. Each tin can is called a **node,** just as each computer or hardware device in a network is a node.

Nodes are connected by a **communications channel** of some sort. The different types of communications channels are shown in the illustration.

Why are there so many different communication channels? Because of the need for *bandwidth,* which refers to the capacity of a communications channel to carry information, and, to some extent, *transmission speed.* Twisted-pair

LEARNING THE lingo

communications channel The physical technology used to link nodes in a network. It may be wires or other types of signals.

wires have limited bandwidth, while fiber optic has extraordinarily great bandwidth. The way most of us recognize bandwidth, or the lack of it, is in the speed at which Web pages load. A modem connected to twisted-pair phone lines loads pages much more slowly than a campus computer connected to a network with coaxial cable. The more complex the information, such as full-motion video, the more bandwidth you need.

What Is Communications Hardware?

Remember that word node? Well, any piece of hardware in a communications channel that is responsible for passing stuff through the network is a node. The most common node is a computer, whether a PC or a supercomputer. A computer that handles traffic and dispenses files or information is usually called a **server.** Computers that host Web pages are servers.

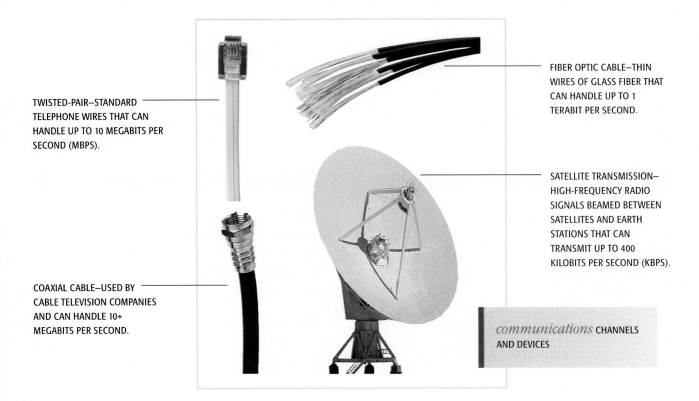

TWISTED-PAIR—STANDARD TELEPHONE WIRES THAT CAN HANDLE UP TO 10 MEGABITS PER SECOND (MBPS).

FIBER OPTIC CABLE—THIN WIRES OF GLASS FIBER THAT CAN HANDLE UP TO 1 TERABIT PER SECOND.

SATELLITE TRANSMISSION—HIGH-FREQUENCY RADIO SIGNALS BEAMED BETWEEN SATELLITES AND EARTH STATIONS THAT CAN TRANSMIT UP TO 400 KILOBITS PER SECOND (KBPS).

COAXIAL CABLE—USED BY CABLE TELEVISION COMPANIES AND CAN HANDLE 10+ MEGABITS PER SECOND.

communications CHANNELS AND DEVICES

PC & You : *UNDERSTANDING BANDWIDTH AND TRANSMISSION SPEED*

Bandwidth refers to the capacity of a communications channel to carry data or information. Bandwidth is measured in cycles per second, or Hertz (abbreviated Hz). Voice bandwidth is not much of an issue; the frequency range of the human voice is quite narrow, about 300–3,000 Hz. But what happens when a friend tries to play music with a frequency range of 20–20,000 Hz over the phone for you? Chances are it doesn't sound quite as good as your stereo.

Bandwidth is measured in two ways. The first is the number of messages the communications channel can carry; whether voice or data—the more, the better. This is distinct from transmission speed because the type of message determines the number of messages a channel can carry and how quickly the message can be delivered.

For example, a credit card authorization request is typically 1kbit, or 1,000 bits, and takes only an instant. However, if you are downloading a graphic image or a full-motion video clip from the Web, it could range upward of several megabits and take minutes or even hours. In such cases, files are often compacted using data compression techniques to save space and speed up transmission. A commonly used program for data compression is WinZip.

The second way bandwidth is measured is by the nature and quality of the signal. Data must have a very, very clear channel; what you hear as noise on the phone line can completely corrupt a data transmission. Coaxial cable is affected by inclement weather, and falling autumn leaves can downgrade microwave transmissions. Imagine the significance of this to a bank that is electronically transferring several billion dollars. In addition, full-motion video used in multimedia applications requires very high bandwidth channel capabilities. Thus the communications channel must be as wide and as clean as possible to accommodate a large number of complex signals.

In order to have fast transmission speed, you need to have both the host computer (such as your ISP) and the client computer (your computer) using the same communications standards. If you have a 56Kbps (that's 56,000 bits per second) modem but your ISP only has 28.8Kbps modems, then you won't be able to connect at the higher speed. Transmission speed is measured in kilobits per second (kbps) or gigabits per second (gbps), tending toward the higher speeds all the time. Wideband transmission has the highest speeds, 19,200 baud to 500Kbps or higher. It is for commercial grade channels used in business, finance, the government, and in particular the World Wide Web. As the Web grows more graphical and delivers more streaming video and sound, bandwidth and transmission speed will continue to be an issue.

Communications devices aren't necessarily able to take full advantage of communications channel bandwidth:

Communication Device	Bandwidth Speed
Analog modem	33.6–56Kbps
DSL modem	128Kbps to 384Kbps
T1 (campus)	1.544Mbps
Cable modem	2 Mbps

E-Notes
The all-digital network.

DSL is the next great communications channel, because it's all-digital. DSL stands for *Digital Subscriber Line,* a service gaining great popularity with people who are on the Internet a lot, like people working from home. DSL gives you two services on the same line, regular voice telephone calls plus Internet access all the time—you're always connected. DSL runs at speeds up to 1.5 Mbps using standard twisted-pair phone lines. You'll need a special DSL modem and maybe some other hardware, plus a custom phone line connection. If you don't have DSL in your area, you probably will soon.

The computer that uses services and information from servers is usually called a **client.** If you are using your PC to surf the Web, you are termed the client.

Some other types of communications hardware include the following:

- *Bridge.* Connects similar networks together.
- *Controller.* Routes data among different devices.
- *Hub.* Handles incoming dialup calls and forwards them.

- *Multiplexer.* Splits one channel so that many nodes can use it.

- *Router.* Determines where to send or forward data on the network.

- *Switch.* Selects the path for where to send data. Sometimes combined with a router.

What Is Communications Software? The three most important kinds of communications software are the network operating system, the server software, and the client software.

A network of computers needs a *network operating system,* or NOS, in order to operate properly. It makes it pos-

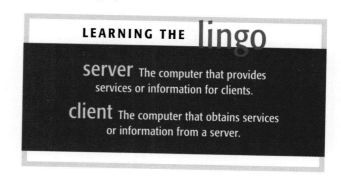

LEARNING THE lingo

server The computer that provides services or information for clients.

client The computer that obtains services or information from a server.

sible to share different hardware, such as a printer, as well as applications and files. The NOS also manages all the people on the network and insures that there is proper security so unauthorized people can't use it.

NOVELL NETWARE IS A NETWORK OPERATING SYSTEM (NOS).

MICROSOFT WINDOWS 2000 SERVER SUPPORTS THE INTERNET AND WEBSITES.

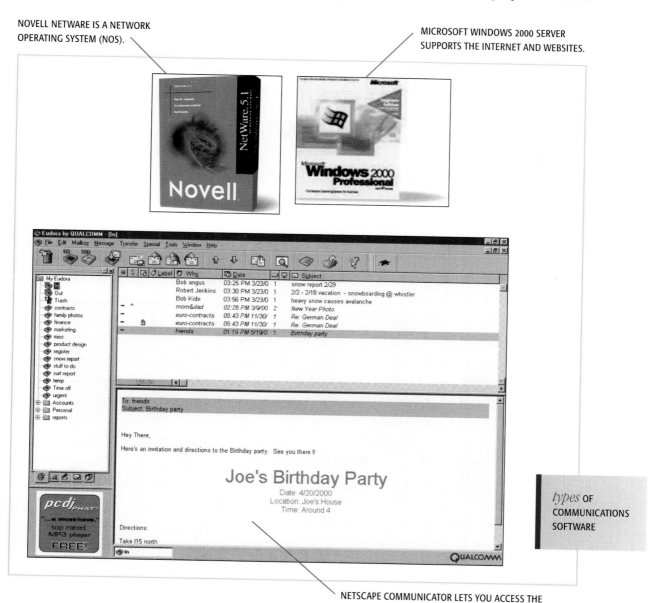

types OF COMMUNICATIONS SOFTWARE

NETSCAPE COMMUNICATOR LETS YOU ACCESS THE NETWORK, VIEW WEB PAGES, AND USE E-MAIL.

E-Notes

Dial-up networking with Windows.

The first thing you must do to connect your PC to a network such as the Internet is set up the software that establishes the connections. In Windows, this is called Dial-Up Networking, or DUN, and it is a utility in the Windows operating system. Windows uses a special utility called a wizard that helps you set up DUN, making it a pretty easy task. It will take you through the following steps:

- Set up your communications hardware. This involves identifying your modem and assuring that it is properly connected.

- Install the Windows TCP/IP protocol and bind it to the Dial-Up Networking adapter. The DUN software does this at your command.

- Enter TCP/IP information. You may need to get this from your ISP.

- Install Dial-Up Networking. Let the software save all the information you have given it and restart your computer.

- Create a connection to your access provider using Dial-Up Networking. This involves typing in the name of the server, the phone number, and your logon name and password.

- Dial your Internet access provider. You should be able to connect and go online.

Server software does pretty much the same thing as the NOS, but only for that particular server or computer. Like an airport traffic controller, server software determines which computers can participate in a network and the proper paths for communications to take.

Client software is what you use to obtain the information and use the services of servers. The two types of client software you're probably most familiar with are the Web browser and e-mail program.

What Is a Network Topology? Like anything else with some complexity to it, a network must have a design. *Topology* defines the layout of computers and other devices and how they are connected. Check out the illustration to see several types of commonly used network designs.

Local Area Networks. For the most part, network topology refers to a **local area network,** or **LAN.** As the name suggests, LANs are set up to allow a small group of people in the same geographic location, such as a dorm, an office, or a small company, to share data,

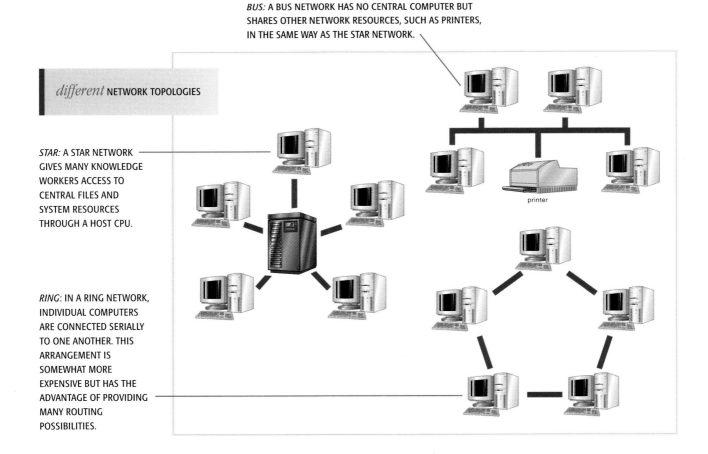

BUS: A BUS NETWORK HAS NO CENTRAL COMPUTER BUT SHARES OTHER NETWORK RESOURCES, SUCH AS PRINTERS, IN THE SAME WAY AS THE STAR NETWORK.

different NETWORK TOPOLOGIES

STAR: A STAR NETWORK GIVES MANY KNOWLEDGE WORKERS ACCESS TO CENTRAL FILES AND SYSTEM RESOURCES THROUGH A HOST CPU.

RING: IN A RING NETWORK, INDIVIDUAL COMPUTERS ARE CONNECTED SERIALLY TO ONE ANOTHER. THIS ARRANGEMENT IS SOMEWHAT MORE EXPENSIVE BUT HAS THE ADVANTAGE OF PROVIDING MANY ROUTING POSSIBILITIES.

printer

PC & You: BUILD YOUR OWN NETWORK

Networked PCs and laptops give you the ability to share files, printers, Internet access, and peripherals installed on a single PC, such as a CD-ROM or tape backup drive. You'll need only one printer, one modem, and one phone line. If you like to play games, many offer a multiplayer option so you can play over your personal network.

If networking your home computers sounds like a good idea, buy a LAN connection kit. They're quite inexpensive. Ethernet LAN kits usually come with two network interface cards, cabling, and a four-port hub that you need to connect everything to. Lay out all the hardware and follow the instructions for what to connect and when to run the installation software.

Windows must be able to recognize your network interface card, or NIC. Most new network adapters follow the Windows Plug and Play specification, but if Windows doesn't detect it, you can go to the Add New Hardware icon in the Control Panel. Once it has recognized the card, Windows will automatically install IPX/SPX, the default networking protocol that allows your PCs to communicate. Windows also installs the network requester, or client, software. You'll also want to install the TCP/IP protocol to get on the Internet.

Before your networked PCs can share resources, you must install the resource-sharing software on each system. Follow the instructions in the Network applet's Configuration tab and then restart the system. Lastly, go to Windows Explorer and highlight the drive or printer you want to share. Click the right mouse button to choose the Sharing option and then name the resource. You can pick practical names, such as Epson Color Printer or Notebook PC, or you can name them after Star Wars characters. Now all the resources will appear in the Network Neighborhood folder where they can be accessed by others. You're ready to network!

home NETWORKING KITS INCLUDE ALL THE HARDWARE, COMMUNICATIONS CHANNEL WIRING, AND SOFTWARE YOU NEED TO NETWORK YOUR HOME OR OFFICE COMPUTERS. WINDOWS NETWORKING NEIGHBORHOOD CAN ALSO BE USED FOR THE SOFTWARE.

LEARNING THE lingo

local area network A network that enables a small group of people fairly close to one another—for example in one building or dorm—to share hardware, software, and information resources using networking.

programs, and hardware resources. A LAN may use any of the three types of networks—star, bus or ring.

5.3 UNDERSTANDING E-BUSINESS AND E-COMMERCE

E-business is an umbrella term that refers to the use of computer networks to improve a firm's operating performance and create additional value for customers. The ability to link operations to the Internet and the Web is essential.

Dell and a few other groundbreakers have been perfecting the direct-to-the-customer sales model. A key component of this model is e-commerce supported by state-of-the-art supply chain management. One of Dell's

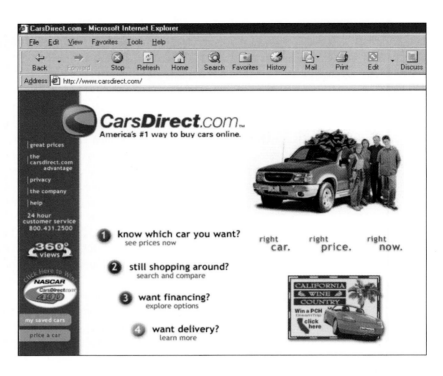

first moves was to cease selling through the retail bricks-and-mortar distribution channel as the company was not making any money at it. As Michael Dell says in his book, *Direct from Dell*, "The real value was that [exiting retail] forced all of our people to focus 100% on the direct model. That single-mindedness was a powerful unifying force."

E-commerce refers to buying goods and services over the World Wide Web. There are two types of e-commerce:

• Business-to-consumer (B-to-C) e-commerce involves companies selling products or services to individuals.

• Business-to-business e-commerce (B-to-B) involves companies selling products or services to other businesses.

E-commerce pioneers are doing the following:

1. Gathering data online and integrating it with internal sales, marketing, and customer service databases to better understand the customer.

2. Identifying the most valuable customers and creating promotion and service strategies to please them, such as customized, password-protected web sites, online catalogues, and other special services.

3. Offering web-based customer support, such as help wizards, sales/buying agents, dedicated trading exchanges and, perhaps, information about competing products

4. Making online service more friendly and offering real-time account information.

5. Using the Web to share information.

E-Notes
Network gaming.

One of the hottest online activities is games, and one of the greatest sites for gaming information is IDG's GameProWorld at www.games.com. Reviews of every kind of electronic or computer game, including Nintendo, Sony Playstation, and PC, often link you to websites where you can play the game or try out demos. You'll also get tips and strategies for ways to play your favorite games better, as well as freebies and the opportunity to go interactive with your own reviews.

talking*issues*

HOW TO KEEP YOUR PC SYSTEM SECURE

Whenever you're connected to the Internet, you're vulnerable to an unauthorized hacker gaining access to your system. Here are some simple precautions:

▶▶ Keep people from physically accessing your computer. Hackers gain access to your computer's contents via a "back door" that allows them to control your computer from a network.

▶▶ Don't open e-mail attachments from strangers or from anyone if you have any concern about what they contain. An attachment can contain a virus, or may make it possible for a hacker to gain access to your system.

▶▶ Run a monitor program that checks the security of your connection to the Internet, such as ShieldsUp.

▶▶ Whenever you are conducting an e-commerce transaction, make sure the merchant is using secure systems to protect your password and credit card information.

▶▶ Be careful who you grant permission to "cookies" to. You may end up getting a rash of pornographic e-mail from Guatemala.

▶▶ Set your browser's security setting to at least medium.

HACKING WEBSITES

In early 2000, a number of websites were hit by a "denial of service" attack. A denial-of-service attack floods a system with hits so that it cannot provide its usual service. Such attacks are not typical and are most likely conducted by experienced, professional computer experts with massive computer resources. Hacking is nothing new, however, and has been going on trivially, accidentally, and intentionally for years.

People who intrude, or break in to computer systems, are sometimes inappropriately called hackers. A *hacker* is someone who demonstrates great skill in programming and working with computers. A computer abuser is an intruder, sometimes called a *cracker,* who is either behaving unethically or illegally in the use of computer systems. Intruders interfere with computer systems owned or operated by others.

Steven Levy, in his 1984 book *Hackers: Heroes of the Computer Revolution* set forth the following "Hacker Ethic":

▶▶ Access to computers should be unlimited and total.

▶▶ All information should be free.

▶▶ Mistrust authority; promote decentralization.

▶▶ Hackers should be judged by their hacking, not by bogus criteria such as degrees, age, race, or position.

▶▶ You create art and beauty on a computer.

▶▶ Computers can change your life for the better.

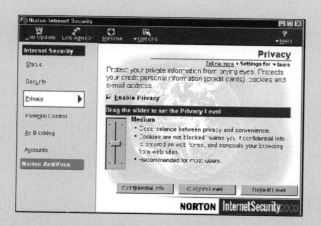

Norton INTERNET SECURITY 2000 ELIMINATES VIRUSES, PROVIDES DEFENSE AGAINST CRACKERS, MANAGES INTERNET ACCESS, AND SAFEGUARDS YOUR PERSONAL INFORMATION

chapter REVIEW

DO-IT-YOURSELF SUMMARY

1. Communications technology, from the computer standpoint, involves _____ signals.

2. When two or more computers are connected, they form a _____.

3. A _____ can be a printer, computer, or other communications device.

4. Network devices are connected via a _____ _____.

5. _____ provide services or information across a network to _____.

6. Networks require their own special _____ _____ _____.

7. The design of a network is called a _____.

8. The three main types of _____ _____ network design are _____, _____, and _____.

9. _____ involves using a computer network to improve business performance.

10. Buying and selling across the Web is called _____.

11. It's possible for a _____ to gain access to your computer.

KEY TERMS REVIEW

a. analog
b. client
c. communications channel
d. computer network
e. digital
f. local area network
g. node
h. server

___ 1. A signal that changes in tone, pitch, and volume.

___ 2. A steady-stream signal that does not change.

___ 3. Software, hardware, and communications channels.

___ 4. Any hardware device connected to a network.

___ 5. The wiring or means of conveying signals between computers.

___ 6. A computer that delivers information.

___ 7. A computer that receives information.

___ 8. A geographically small network.

ANSWERS: 1. digital; 2. network; 3. node; 4. channel; 5. servers, clients; 6. network operating system; 7. topology; 8. local area, star, bus, ring; 9. E-business; 10. e-commerce; 11. hacker.

ANSWERS: 1. a; 2. e; 3. d; 4. g; 5. c; 6. h; 7. b, 8. f.

KEY CONCEPTS REVIEW

a. bandwidth
b. communications infrastructure
c. cracker
d. digital subscriber line (DSL)
e. e-business
f. e-commerce
g. hacker
h. network operating system
i. networking
j. topology
k. transmission speed

____ 1. Computers when they are communicating.

____ 2. The networking that connects networks.

____ 3. A communication channel's capacity.

____ 4. A communication channel's rate of data transfer.

____ 5. An all-digital network.

____ 6. The essential system software for a network.

____ 7. Name for a network design.

____ 8. Using the Internet to improve business procedures.

____ 9. Buying and selling over the Web.

____ 10. A skilled computer person.

____ 11. An unethical or lawbreaking computer person.

HANDS-ON EXERCISES

This exercise is designed to help you determine what is most useful to you about using the Internet, including e-mail and the Web. Plan to spend an hour or more with the questions, exploring each one online until you have an answer.

1. After spending _____ hours researching online information services, I have concluded that I (do) (do not) need them to improve my work.

2. I have concluded that the only thing I need is _____ (e-mail, the Web, chat, etc.).

3. List the online information services you feel would be most beneficial in your work. Be as specific as you can.

4. What aspect of your work pertains to online applications?

5. How would your work be enhanced by using online applications?

6. What specific types of online information would you like to obtain, and how would it be used in your studies or work?

7. Describe how the quality of the information you work with and produce now would be improved with the value added by online information?

8. How would you share the information you obtain with others?

9. Explain how your personal productivity would be enhanced through the use of online information services.

10. Which online information services are of particular interest or usefulness to you?

ANSWERS: 1. i; 2. b; 3. a; 4. k; 5. d; 6. h; 7. j; 8. e; 9. f; 10. g; 11. c.

photo **credits**

CHAPTER 1

Page 2: Shatner/bridge of the Enterprise, **Motion Picture and Television Photo Archive.**

Page 10: Current PC, Courtesy of Compaq.

Page 11: Person designing a multimedia application, **AP/Wide World Photos.**

Page 12: Fenton and Bliss, freelance web designers, **Courtesy of Hireability.com.**

Page 13: Burton Snowboard, **Courtesy of Jager Di Paola Kemp Design.**

CHAPTER 2

Page 22: Tim Berners-Lee, **AP/Wide World Photos.**

CHAPTER 4

Page 59: Intel Concept PC, **Courtesy of Intel Corporation.**

Page 59–60: MacIntosh PowerMac G4, **Courtesy of Apple Computer, Inc.**

Page 60: Gateway Profile II, **Courtesy of Gateway, Inc.**

Page 60: Sony VAIO Slimtop PCV-L620, **Courtesy of Sony Electronics.**

Page 64 (clockwise from top left): Cyrix Joshua, **Courtesy of Viatech.** IBM PowerPC G3, **Courtesy of Motorola, Inc.** Motorola G4, **Courtesy of Motorola, Inc.** Intel Pentium III, **Courtesy of Intel Corporation.** AMD Athlon, **Courtesy of Advanced Micro Devices, Inc.**

Page 65: Photo of SIMMS, **Courtesy of PNY Technologies.**

Page 71: (left) DVD, **Scott Goodwin Photography.** (right) Zip disk, **Courtesy of Iomega Corporation.**

CHAPTER 5

Page 76: Al Gore, **AP/ Wide World Photos.**

Page 81: Twisted pair, coaxial cable, fiber optic cable, satellite transmission, **© PhotoDisc, Inc.**

Page 83 (clockwise from top left): NOS (Novell NOS) box shot, **Courtesy of Novell Corporation.** Server box shot Windows 2000, **Courtesy of Microsoft, Inc.** Eudora screen capture, **Courtesy of Qualcomm Eudora Products.**

Page 85: LAN kit package, **Courtesy of Intel Corporation.**

Page 87: Norton Internet Security 2000 package, **Courtesy of Symantec Corporation.**

index